ADVANCE PRAISE

"For anyone who dreams big and has the talent it takes to go great places, but must dig deep and break the cycles of the past in order to achieve true happiness."

—Meredith Land, news anchor and reporter, NBC TV, Dallas-Fort Worth, Texas

"'Girl in the Spotlight' is nothing less than a how-to on saving your life."

—Nikki Hardin, founder and former publisher, Skirt! magazine

"'Girl in the Spotlight' is about one woman learning to let go of expectations and begin to process childhood loss so that she can finally begin building a life that is both authentic and fulfilling."

—Kate Hopper, author of "Ready for Air" and "Use Your Words"

"Angie Mizzell's vulnerable and direct writing style captures the growing tension between the desires of the heart and soul, versus the demands of our best-laid plans."

—Ann Imig, founder of "Listen to Your Mother" nationwide storytelling series

"One of those books you read and immediately hand off to a friend because you know they need to read it too."

"'Girl in the Spotlight' leaves you looking in the mirror asking the most important question of all: What's in your heart and what's really most important in that life you live every day?"

"An overdue permission slip to release the things that no longer serve you and rediscover who you are without the burden of an outdated dream."

"A poignant story about discovering what home really is."

Girl in the Spotlight

a memoir

ANGIE MIZZELL

PUBLISH **HER**™

GIRL IN THE SPOTLIGHT

© Copyright 2023 Angie Mizzell

This book is memoir. It reflects the author's present recollections of experiences over time. Some names and characteristics may have been changed, some events may have been compressed, and some dialogue may have been recreated.

Company and/or product names referenced in this book may be logos, trade names, trademarks, and/or registered trademarks, and are the property of their respective owners.

ISBN: 979-8-9883444-8-3 (Softcover)
ISBN: 979-8-9883444-7-6 (Hardcover)
ISBN: 979-8-9883444-9-0 (E-book)
Printed in the United States of America
First Printing: 2023

Published by Publish Her, LLC
6726 Walker Street
St. Louis Park, MN 55426
www.publishherpress.com

PUBLISH **HER**™

This book is for the one who carries pain from the past and longs to be free. I wrote this to remind you that you are stronger than you think. You have the power to break the cycle. You are loved, you are enough and you are not alone.

Also, it's for Shawn, Dillon, Blake and Cate. You make everything worth it. You make it all make sense.

PART ONE

DREAMS

You could say I was born to be on TV. Once, my mom told me the story of how she named me. She said the inspiration struck while watching an episode of the 1970s show "Police Woman." "I saw Angie Dickinson's name flash across the television screen, and I liked the way it looked." Angie. I was still in the womb, but she already knew that I was a girl. "I could just feel it," she said. Even then, she imagined big things for my life. She always said I could do anything.

And because she said it, I believed it.

Mom got pregnant with me when she was just 17, a senior in high school. She and my father, John, who was two years older, had planned to get married in June. Instead, they made up an excuse about why they needed to push up the wedding date, and Mom walked down the aisle in May, weeks before graduation and weeks before the baby bump became obvious. My grandmother knew about me, but my grandfather didn't. After the wedding, when my mom finally told her father that she was expecting, he slammed his fist on the kitchen counter so hard it rattled the dishes in the cabinets.

My grandfather Bobby was a retired Army paratrooper; he'd married my grandmother Frances when he was 19 and she was 17. My mom was born a year later, and her brother arrived five years after that. So Bobby and Frances were still quite young—in their mid-30s—when they learned that they were about to become grandparents. But Mom was a daddy's girl, and he eventually came around.

Mom says I gave them all a reason to be happy—hopeful—and my birth was a celebration. Moments after I arrived, my grandmother ran down the hallway of the maternity ward shouting, "It's a girl! It's a girl!" as she waved a roll of dimes in the air. Then she closed herself into a phone booth and called everyone she knew.

"You were an accident but not a mistake," my mom always said, and she somehow, miraculously, convinced me of this, even as she insisted that I wouldn't take the path that she did. My life would be different. Better. I'd go to college and have a career. I wouldn't date, much less marry, anyone who acted jealous or treated me like a possession. Mom learned that lesson the hard way.

✦

Channel 5 has always been the No. 1 television news station in Charleston, the coastal city in South Carolina where I grew up. When I was 6 years old, I spotted Channel

5's main sportscaster in a department store. He smiled and said hello and I was so in awe I couldn't speak. A few years later, while having dinner at Pizza Hut with my small fry cheerleading team, I saw the station's meteorologist sitting in a booth with his family. I slipped him a note written on a napkin asking, "Why is the sky blue?" When he came to the table and offered an explanation—something about molecules and the sun—my friends and I giggled, like self-conscious preteen girls do.

I would go on to become the first person in my family to graduate from college, and soon after, I went to work for that same news station myself. I was officially part of the team. The Live 5 News Team. Those local celebrities were my co-workers, guests at my wedding and my friends.

It felt surreal.

✦

Shawn and I met in a television production class at the University of South Carolina in Columbia and started dating during our junior year. After graduation, we worked together at the same news station in Columbia and both got jobs in Savannah before finally moving back to my hometown of Charleston to work for Live 5 News. It always happened the same way: I got the job first and then the boss would find out about Shawn and hire him on the spot. Each time, we shook our heads in disbelief. TV news was a tough, competitive business, and we couldn't have predicted that our career paths would line up so easily, as if a divine hand were pulling the strings, offering up opportunities, and snapping the pieces of our future into place.

In the first year of living and working in Charleston, things progressed quickly. Shawn moved up the ranks in the production department to director of the 10 p.m. newscast. He proposed marriage. I got promoted from reporter to morning anchor.

I was living a dream.

✦

During my senior year of high school, I joined the journalism club. Students took turns hosting the school's morning announcements, which were broadcast on classroom televisions and consisted of top headlines like, "Lunch for today is Salisbury steak." One day a camera crew from Channel 5 came to the school and did a story about us, and the short feature segment aired on the news that night. There was a lot of buzz around campus the next day: Did you see the news? Our school was on TV!

After our 30 seconds of fame, my teachers stopped me in the hallways between classes to tell me I was doing a good job. Some said I should consider a career in TV news. "You could be the next Nancy O'Dell," one of them said. I lit up, the praise stirring butterflies that made me feel both excited and like I might throw up.

Nancy anchored the morning show at Channel 2, another local station in Charleston. Each day before school, I'd turn on the television and study her as she talked to the camera. I wondered how—wondered if—I could ever be like her. She had blonde hair, just like me. Unlike me, she was tall, poised and polished—a former Miss South Carolina, an actual beauty queen. I was barely 5-foot-3 and a cheerleader, much more skilled at hip-hop dancing in sneakers than walking gracefully in a formal gown and heels. But I couldn't stop watching her and hoping that my teachers were right.

As I went off to college and began my career, I paid close attention as Nancy moved from anchoring a morning show in Charleston, to a news station in Miami, to "Access Hollywood" in Los Angeles. Her path became my definition of success.

✦

There's a photo of Shawn and me on our wedding day sitting in a horse-drawn carriage parked outside a 200-year-old church in Charleston, the skirt of my antique white dress spilling out, and the flowers in my bouquet trailing. The image—which was published in Charleston magazine—looked like a fairy tale. Minutes before it was taken, a Channel 5 camera crew waited outside, and later that night, the whole scene ran on the evening news.

"Sorry guys, Live 5's morning anchor Angie Mizzell is off the market," our friend and co-worker Gurnal read from the anchor desk. "Earlier this evening, she married our News at 10 director Shawn Moffatt, and our Channel 5 family was there to congratulate them." The video clip was followed by interviews with the main anchor team wishing us well. My favorite was from the morning show meteorologist who shared my 3:30 a.m. wakeup calls, admitting his jealousy that I was jetting off to Jamaica for the honeymoon and would get to sleep in for an entire week.

He had a right to be jealous. That middle-of-the-night alarm was brutal. There was no getting used to it. There was only an understanding that if I followed the routine—don't hit snooze, go straight to the shower, brush my teeth, dry my hair, put on my suit and grab a Diet Coke on the way out the door—when I arrived at the station at 4 a.m., I'd be awake.

My mom made it home from the wedding reception in time to record the news on the VCR, and when Shawn and I returned from our honeymoon a week later, we sat on her living room floor and watched the tape.

There were so many things about my job in news that were far from glamorous—the long hours, always working against the clock, covering murders and tragedies—but now, as Shawn and I viewed the highlights of our wedding day, all of that seemed to fall away. I couldn't believe I'd arrived at this place, my name flashing across the television screen just as my mom imagined. It's possible that I'd finally achieved everything she ever wanted for me.

But I wanted more. Shawn and I were on a trajectory. As much as we both loved Charleston, it was never supposed to be our last stop.

✦

After our wedding was highlighted on the news, I got recognized in public more often, reminiscent of the days when I slipped a note to the meteorologist at Pizza Hut. People stared at me in Walmart. Strangers would strike up a conversation as Shawn and I searched for a movie at the video store. At work, people quickly returned my phone calls requesting interviews. It gave me the confidence boost I needed to start thinking about our next move.

I put together a demo reel on VHS tape showcasing my best anchoring and reporting and sent it to a well-known talent placement agency—the same agency that had represented Nancy O'Dell. I'd been told by my journalism professors that it only took three seconds for the industry gatekeepers to decide whether to continue watching my tape or hit eject. Right there in the middle of the post office, I kissed the package before dropping it in the slot.

Two weeks later, I got a call from an agent, Andrew, who offered to represent me and help me find my next opportunity. I couldn't believe I'd been picked out of a stack. I couldn't believe it happened so quickly.

I told him about how I'd watched Nancy O'Dell make a big leap from Charleston to Miami to Los Angeles. I told him that one day, I wanted to host a national entertainment news show like "Access Hollywood," just like her. He didn't hesitate. He said we could do it. After we hung up, I sat in my cubicle and looked around the busy newsroom, stunned. The dream was becoming real.

I thought the life I was creating for myself was indeed the path to happiness. I couldn't see how my sense of love, belonging and self-worth had gotten tangled up in my ambition. As a journalist I made a living telling other people's stories, but soon, I'd arrive at a crossroads and have no choice but begin to examine my own.

FAMILY PORTRAIT

When I was a baby and my mom and my father, John, were still together, we lived in a brick ranch-style house with green shutters. Photo albums tell the story of how my mom and I spent our days outside in the sunshine while John was at work. In one image I'm wearing a white sundress, swinging in the backyard. In another I'm standing in a plastic swimming pool and wearing a red-checkered bikini. My wispy hair is secured with a barrette, and I'm holding a garden hose, water drizzling out. More snapshots show me sleeping on my parents' bed—my favorite place to nap—my arm wrapped around a baby doll. I'm not sure if I remember any of this, or if the photos bring the scenes to life in my mind. But one thing I know: With my mom, I felt safe.

There are other images, ones never documented in photos, but still, they're etched in my memory. I'm in the living room, or perhaps the hallway, and I'm hanging onto my mom's leg and screaming through tears, "Mommy! Mommy!" John is shouting and grabbing her, and I'm trying to protect her, trying to be her safe place, trying to make it stop.

I have one good childhood memory, a vivid memory, of John. We are at the Battery in downtown Charleston, a historic park on the edge of the peninsula on the harbor, with plenty of green space for children to run around and climb on Civil War cannons. We were running around and around a monument. He was just ahead of me, but going faster, and suddenly he was out of sight, as if he'd disappeared into thin air. A few seconds later, he'd reappear. I never saw him come or go. We'd play this game over and over, and I'd laugh, fascinated by this magic.

Other memories of John, the ones full of rage, come in flashes. I'm following my mom into the Piercing Pagoda at the mall, announcing that I want to get my ears pierced too. The pounding of bathwater. More yelling. My shirt catching the earring of my newly pierced lobe as John yanks it over my head. Blood. The bath towel being pressed to my ear. He said he didn't mean to hurt me, but I couldn't escape his anger, spilling out everywhere. I mostly tried to be very good, never knowing what might set off his explosive temper.

He started hitting Mom after they got married. On better days, John was polite and charming, making it difficult for my mom to leave him and for my grandparents to fully accept that there was a dark side. But as the situation escalated, they couldn't continue to look the other way. My grandmother saw Mom's bruises, and when I was 3, she and my grandfather scrounged up a few hundred dollars to help Mom file for divorce.

After the divorce, John got a job in Alaska and disappeared from my life. Mom and I moved to an apartment where the front doors were inside the building, like a hotel. There, I see myself wearing yellow water wings and floating in the community swimming pool. Mom says I liked to be the center of attention, holding court with the young men also hanging out at the pool. I vaguely remember that, and I wonder if they were chitchatting with me to impress my mom. In my mind's eye, she's the only one in focus, so young and beautiful with her blonde hair and bright face, nearby on a lounge chair, watching me, smiling.

When we went places, I rode shotgun in the passenger seat of her red Chevette (before children were required by law to ride in the back), serenading her with the latest Rod Stewart song about heart and soul. I was, of course, too young to understand what a lover was, I just knew that I loved her. That year, she gave me the record for Valentine's Day.

"You know what this says?" she asked, pointing to the words on the label. "It says, 'you're in my heart.'"

✦

Oh, how I wished those moments—the playing, the swimming, the singing—could have been our life, every day.

But Mom needed to work. Her divorce attorney made some calls and soon she had a job as a receptionist at another law firm in downtown Charleston.

When Mom dropped me off at my grandparents' house on her first day of work, I sobbed with arms outstretched and begged her not to go. My grandmother sat on the bar stool at the end of the kitchen counter and held me. She rocked me and kept telling me it would be all right until I stopped crying.

And I adjusted, especially since my grandparents' house on Marilyn Drive felt like home to me. Their house felt like home to everyone. The garage door was always open and it never once held a car. Instead, it was set up like a patio, with green AstroTurf-like carpet; a round table and chairs in the front for conversations over glasses of sweet tea and cans of beer; a picnic table in the back for buffet-style Sunday dinners. On New Year's Eve, or the occasional Saturday night, the garage became a dance floor.

When family and friends stopped by to visit, or neighbors popped over to borrow a cup of milk or a couple of eggs, they entered through the garage and tapped on the screen door that led to the small galley kitchen, letting themselves in by announcing, "Knock-knock!" and congregating around the counter. The kitchen opened to the family room, which we called the den, and the TV was always on.

The house also had a formal living room, with green shag carpet my grandmother would groom with a rake to make it stand up. I was rarely allowed in there because I'd leave footprints in the matted shag. The few times I did venture into the living room, it was to study the photo albums stuffed in the end table cabinets; when I was done, I immediately fluffed the carpet to cover my tracks. The other rule was to never answer the front door. We only opened the front door on Halloween night, when my grandmother greeted the neighborhood trick-or-treaters with pre-assembled bags of candy labeled with their names written in her fancy cursive. If the front doorbell rang at any other time, we ignored it. We knew it was someone soliciting. And, when friends and family phoned, my grandmother instructed them to "give the signal": Call once, hang up and call again. If the orange rotary dial phone hanging on the kitchen wall rang and the caller didn't give the signal, we didn't answer, suspecting it was a bill collector.

My grandfather would sometimes pore over the checkbook and fuss at my grandmother, "Frances, when you get to zero, you're supposed to fucking stop!" Stories like these got woven into our family narrative, tales I'd hear the adults repeat again and again, laughing so hard it brought tears. At night, my grandfather would sit at the kitchen counter and drink Budweiser until he passed out. Sometimes, I'd help my grandmother put him to bed and he'd pretend to collapse to the floor, coherent enough to know what he was doing and drunk enough to think it was funny. My grandfather was lovable and happy when he had a buzz; my grandmother would sometimes get mad at these games but never for long. On payday Fridays, as we all got ready to go out to eat, he'd pretend to cut himself shaving and emerge from the bathroom bleeding from his face; he continued this act even after we quickly realized the blood was actually ketchup. At the restaurant, my baby doll sat in the highchair and my grandfather would offer her the food on his fork.

Mom struggled to pay the rent at our hotel-like apartment, and just before I turned 4, we moved in with my grandparents. There was never enough money, but I rarely felt the effects of it. Some nights, I was the only one they could afford to feed dinner, but I didn't know it at the time. I enjoyed my box of Church's fried chicken with delight. I was clean, clothes pressed, hair curled. I was loved, adored. This love was a magical shield that blinded me to the dysfunction, adult worries and depression pressing down on their wide-open hearts.

For my fifth birthday, my grandparents bought me a pink birthstone ring. Not long afterward, I lost it. My friends and I had been rolling down a hill and it fell off. I was devastated when I looked at my hand and the ring was gone. The next day, my grandmother went back to the hill with a garden rake. She combed through the grass and dirt until she found it. When she picked me up from school that afternoon, she smiled like a fairy godmother as she handed me the ring.

Of them all, my grandmother was the one. The one who felt invincible to me.

She spent her days cleaning the house, cooking our meals, talking on the phone, watching soap operas and taking afternoon naps on the couch. I was fine to be right there underfoot or playing outside with the kids across the street. My grandfather worked for Frito-Lay and sometimes he got to drive the delivery truck home. He'd let me crawl inside and eat Moon Pies. Later he converted the covered patio behind the house into an auto body shop. Only one neighbor complained, the one we never spoke to anyway. I'd sit on the sofa in the den and listen to the comforting buzz of the sander vibrating through the windows. My mom's younger brother, my uncle Bobby, taught me how to ride a bike and took me to the gas station after school to get Icees.

In those days, my grandparents' house on Marilyn Drive shaped everything I came to believe about home. Home was constant. It offered a sense of stability and security. Home was a place to gather, to celebrate, to love and be loved. Home was a safe place to fall.

INVITATION

News is a tough business. Even though I'd achieved something I never thought possible—becoming the morning anchor at Charleston's top news station at age 25—it wasn't all spotlights and accolades.

I once fled the morning meeting in tears after the news director told me the story that I'd covered about the safety of the rides at the Coastal Carolina Fair was "the worst piece of crap he'd ever seen." He wasn't wrong. The story was a fluff piece at best. I'd been too timid to ask tough questions. That day, a producer followed me to the makeup room and locked the door behind her. She grabbed me by the shoulders, looked me straight in the eyes and said, "Everyone goes through this. When I first started, I was terrified to open the morning paper, worried I'd missed an important story. One day you'll read the front page and realize you've scooped them. You won't even watch the other stations because you'll know you did it better. It gets easier. I promise."

When I returned to the newsroom, our education reporter winked at me and said, "You're in the club now."

I did my best to take it in stride. I told myself I was just paying my dues until I'd gained enough experience to move on to my next job, another steppingstone to Los Angeles.

Not long after I signed the contract with my agent, the news director was arrested—accused of embezzling money from the station—and taken away in handcuffs. I'd worked the morning shift and had already gone home for the day when Shawn called me and told what happened. I drove back to work to find the entire news team gathered in shock. The news director's abrupt departure left us with mixed emotions, but there was no time to process. Channel 5 had become its own top story and we snapped into action, reporting on the scandal along with our competitors. We did our jobs, just the way our boss had taught us, and we suspected that made him proud.

Rita, Channel 5's general manager, took over running the newsroom in the interim. The energy behind the scenes at Channel 5 shifted in a noticeable way—still bustling, but less frantic. Both classy and sexy, Rita possessed a motherly quality that radiated love and power at the same time. She walked and talked with ease. She commanded respect and attention. When she entered the room, we stopped. When she spoke, we listened. I was drawn to Rita. Everyone was.

Once, when a Category 5 hurricane threatened Charleston, Rita invited employees' families to spend the night at the station because Channel 5 had generators and the building was constructed to withstand extremely high winds. While we worked to keep the nonstop newscast on the air, grandparents, children and pets (even guinea pigs) roamed the building. The storm spared Charleston and The Post and Courier wrote a feature story about Rita and the hurricane party happening at Channel 5 that night. In the article, the meteorologist's wife said there was a moment when she lost her young daughter and found her sitting on Rita's lap. Rita told the paper, "We were doing our job, but we were doing it in a way that said to both our viewers and our employees, 'No matter what, we'll be there for you.'"

✦

After the news director's arrest, Rita fired some employees and hired new ones. One day during the transition, Rita called me into her office. I'd only had pleasant interactions with her, but I felt nervous as I walked through the building toward her office, wondering what she might want. She led me to her desk, offered me a chair and took a seat across from me.

"Angie," she said, "I wanted to tell you how much we love having you on the morning show." She smiled, which was reassuring. Still, I held my breath, anticipating "but here's the bad news." Instead, she said, "We'd like to offer you a three-year contract."

I'm sure I said things like "wow" and "thank you" and "I love anchoring the morning show too," but everything went fuzzy after that. In my wedding album, there was a group photo of the Live 5 News Team, arm-in-arm, stretched across the dance floor. With no clear-cut dividing lines separating life and work, the station had become, quite literally, my second home and family. Still, I'd never seriously considered staying at Channel 5 long term. Until then, I'd only signed one-year work agreements—a simple one-page document. Being presented with a contract came as a surprise and it also made me second-guess my plans to leave so soon. With Rita at the helm, I wondered how it would feel to stay for a while.

The contract didn't offer a huge raise, but it included a small clothing allowance and would be a move from filling out weekly time sheets and calculating overtime to a consistent salary that increased a little each year. It also included a clause that said if I got a job in one of the top 40 television markets in the country, I could leave. It was a generous out. Rita wasn't trying to hold me back or make me decide my entire future right then and there. She was simply picking her team, and she wanted me to be on it. She told me to take some time to think about it. I said thank you and left her office with the unsigned contract in hand.

When I returned to my desk, Mary, Channel 5's senior producer, pulled me aside. She said I should ask Rita to add a line stating that I could be released from my contract if

Shawn got a job outside of Charleston. "You need a Shawn clause," she said. I hadn't considered that. I thanked her for the advice, and when I mentioned the Shawn clause to Rita, she agreed, no problem.

I did, however, have a problem. What about my dream to move to Los Angeles and become the next Nancy O'Dell? What would my agent think? If I accepted the contract, maybe he'd think that I wasn't so serious about my career after all. And what if I didn't sign it? Would that mean that my days at Channel 5 were numbered? I wasn't sure if I wanted to stay for three more years, but I also wasn't ready to say goodbye.

When I got home from work, I called my agent. "Andrew, what do I do?"

To my surprise he said, "Sign the contract. You have nothing to lose. They're offering you job security, but you're not locked in if something big comes up."

I signed the contract. The practical part of me understood all the reasons it made sense. But my agent was wrong about not being locked in. My conversation with Rita had stirred up my childhood yearnings and attachments. After all these years, they still had a grip on me. As I picked up the pen and scribbled my name, I realized that maybe I did have something to lose. The feeling of belonging—and the offer to make it official—had complicated things for me.

BELONGING

I stood in the middle of the living room; my tiny hand clutched a microphone connected to the portable record player Santa had delivered that year. The toy karaoke machine was black and shaped like a jukebox, adorned with psychedelic rainbow stickers to create that 1970s disco effect. And it was big. Three-feet tall, just like me.

I wore my favorite yellow nightgown, long and flowing, and my messy, straight blonde hair hung gloriously free from those pink sponge curlers I was typically required to sleep in. My bare feet sunk into the fuzzy brown carpet. Sunlight streamed in through the sliding glass doors, spotlighting the imaginary stage. I lifted the needle and lowered it to the vinyl; the 45 record crackled as it spun. I bobbed my head to the dramatic pulse of the keyboard, pressed the red button on the microphone to amplify my voice, closed my eyes for effect, and belted out the lyrics to "Cold as Ice."

The fans went wild. Suddenly aware of myself, I opened my eyes and took in my audience: my mom and my grandparents, cheering and clapping. Their glowing faces became a mirror and I saw my reflection in their smiles and their applause. When I looked at myself through their eyes, I knew who I was. I was a rock star. The star of the show.

It was the year I started kindergarten. My mom and I had recently moved out of my grandparents' house and into a townhouse about five minutes away. Our unit was painted white and I thought it looked like a dollhouse. A chair swing hung on the front porch, and when you stood in the driveway and looked up, you could see the yellow Holly Hobbie curtains hanging in my bedroom windows. My mom and I loved that place. I remember her being happy when we were there.

One day, Mom called me to come sit by her on the couch. She wrote out the alphabet on a piece of paper and said, "Today, we're going to learn our ABCs."

The townhouse was close to the elementary school, so close that I could see the playground from the front porch. I was not one of those kids who cried on the first day of school. I was excited to go. On the second day, she let me walk to school with the kids who lived across the street, the door to my classroom just across the grassy field. I'd look back and see my mom standing there, watching me.

✦

One evening, there was a knock on the door and I rushed to answer it. It was a man, looking handsome with his clean-shaven face and dark hair, combed to perfection. When he saw me, he smiled. My heart fluttered at that smile, his kind eyes.

"Hi, I'm Cam."

"I know," I said, giggling.

I ran to get my mom. She'd told me he was coming over. His calm and quiet manner made me feel like he hadn't shown up in my life a few moments ago; he didn't feel new. I loved Cam right away.

My father, John, reappeared that same year, shortly after Mom started dating Cam. I don't recall seeing him much, if at all, since the divorce and his departure for Alaska. Now, he stood in the doorway in a rage, and I hid in the tiny townhouse kitchen, peeking around the corner. He threatened to take me away from Mom if he ever caught Cam spending the night. Then he stormed off.

John was dating someone, too. John, his girlfriend, Mom and Cam had a history; they grew up in the same neighborhoods and went to the same schools. John remarried later that year and the following summer I went to his house for a 10-day visit. On one of my first nights there, he asked me, "Who do you love more? Cam or me?"

I wasn't sure what to say. I went with the first thing that came to me. "I love you both the same," I said. That felt right.

"If that's how you feel," he snapped, "don't ever mention his name around me again." He turned and walked out of the room.

During that visit, I learned to swim in the community pool. I began underwater like a fish, rose to the surface and dog-paddled across the shallow end. Then I got brave and dared to belly flop off the side. John laughed and cheered. Later that day, when I told him I was too scared to dive off the diving board, he threatened to take me back to his house. I stood at the edge, looking down. The water was so far away. I couldn't do it. I needed more time. I wasn't ready.

Finally, he said, "Get your stuff. Let's go." Wrapped in a towel and sliding on my flip-flops, I understood that I wasn't just afraid to dive. I was afraid of him.

One night, after our trip to the pool, I started running a fever. Perhaps I caught a bug. Perhaps it was my body's signal that I was under stress. John's new wife rubbed me down with alcohol and drew me a bath. I was homesick; I missed my mom. But I felt this woman's kindness, and my fever broke.

✦

Even with Mom's steady job at the law firm, she couldn't make ends meet. When I was in first grade, we moved out of the townhouse and back in with my grandparents. My grandfather's mother managed rental properties, so a few months later, we moved into one of her trailers. The trailer park was just outside of the school district and I never mentioned my new address to the teacher. As far as the school was concerned, Mom and I still lived with my grandparents on Marilyn Drive.

Each trailer in the trailer park had a fenced-in yard and our street was a dead end, so I was free to play outside with the neighbor kids. Sometimes Mom would let me walk to the end of the road to check the mail. One afternoon, I saw John's car coming down the street. Instinctively, I turned and ran. This outward display of resistance wasn't typical behavior for me. Even I couldn't believe what I was doing: darting up the steps and inside the trailer, down the long hallway and into my bedroom, sliding on my belly and under the bed and out of sight.

My mom came into my room and coaxed me out. John's wife was with her. We sat together on the edge of my bed, which made me feel safe and brave. I told them I didn't want to go. To my surprise, they said I didn't have to. I'd find out later that Mom went back outside and told John that she'd stop fighting for child support if he'd stay out of our lives. At the time, I didn't know why he suddenly left my life again; I only knew that I felt relieved when I didn't see his car coming down the street anymore.

✦

When I was in second grade, I was the flower girl in Mom and Cam's wedding. After that, we moved to a ranch-style house in a small suburb, which meant a brand-new school, but we were still only about 15 minutes away from my grandparents' house and right around the corner from Cam's parents. I suddenly had one more set of grandparents and a lot more aunts and uncles and cousins. They folded me into their family as if I'd always been a part of it.

We had two golden cocker spaniels that I named Pebbles and Bam Bam and two parakeets, Pete and Pretty Bird. Cam helped me with science projects. I knew I could wait until the last minute and he'd stay up, draping strips of papier-mache over a balloon, spray painting it green, cutting rings out of cardboard boxes and calling it Saturn. He had this unmistakable handwriting, neat and pointy and geometric, which later clued me in that the note from the Easter Bunny was really from him. Sometimes he took me out on the Edisto River in his fishing boat. I'd stare at my line, waiting for the cork to bob up and down, never catching a fish big enough to keep. We didn't talk much, but it was always a comfortable silence. In the background of these memories, there was always music. Sade spinning on the stereo in the kitchen on Saturday mornings; Al Jarreau singing about "Mornin'" in the car on the way to school.

At the dinner table one night in the summer before third grade, I looked around—at the food, at Mom, at Cam, at the three of us sitting together—and was overcome with a sudden awareness that we were a family. I didn't realize anything was missing in my life until it was right there in front of me, and now I wanted it more than anything. Without thinking, or planning or preparing, I said, "Cam, I want you to be my dad."

He turned to face me, eyes wide. He set down his fork. "Are you sure that's what you want?"

"I didn't put her up to this," Mom blurted out, and her stunned expression made me worry that I'd done something wrong. I hadn't discussed it with her, or anyone. I'm not sure if I'd even thought about it until that moment.

Often giggly when I got nervous, I kept my words steady this time. "I want to call you Dad," I said. "I want your parents to be my grandparents, and I want my last name to be Mizzell." It was all clear and obvious to me. I didn't know that it could be like this, would feel like this. Together, at the dinner table, the three of us felt right. I wanted the three of us to stay that way—together—forever.

Since Mom worked as a legal secretary, she had direct access to the attorneys who could make it happen. Cam looked at her and said, "Draw up the papers."

Standing in the lobby of the family courthouse months later, I recognized John's signature when I saw it on the adoption papers. I hadn't seen him since my mom sent him away that day at the trailer park and a pang of loss shot through my body. I understood the gravity of what was happening. Inside the courtroom, I sat at one table and Cam at the other. The judge took his place up front, behind the tall bench. The room seemed so big; everyone seemed so far away. The judge looked at me, pointed to Cam and gently asked, "Do you want this man to be your dad? Is this what you want?"

I giggled and said yes.

✦

I started third grade. When the teacher called the roll on the first day of class, I answered "here" to a last name no one recognized. A row of ponytails snapped around in front of me; jaws dropped.

I addressed the invisible question hanging in the air. "I was adopted," I said. Quiet, but bold. The attention made me feel self-conscious but not ashamed. The teacher smiled and said, "Congratulations," and continued down the roll.

On the playground, my friends, genuinely surprised and confused, wanted to know, "What did you mean when you said you were adopted? Were you an orphan?"

I explained that I still lived with my mom, that my stepdad had adopted me and now I had a family just like them. That's when I understood that there had been something different about me and that being just like them felt important.

AMBIANCE

Not long after I accepted Rita's offer and signed the three-year contract at Channel 5, she hired another producer. The producer and her husband were new to Charleston and had built a house in a neighborhood a few miles from the station. After they moved in, she invited the newsroom staff over for a happy hour.

Along with most of the other 20-somethings who worked at Channel 5, Shawn and I lived in a nearby apartment complex we'd nicknamed "Melrose Place" after a TV drama popular at the time. We joked that our lifestyle was much like the characters in the TV series, our personal and professional lives intertwined. We worked together and played together. We covered the news, went to bars after work and gathered on game days to watch college football. We rang in the new millennium together, working past midnight before gathering back at our apartment where we talked, played games and listened to our co-worker Frank play guitar until the newspaper hit the front door the next morning. So, when we arrived at the producer's two-story home on a cul-de-sac—complete with a pair of palm trees illuminated by spotlights in the front yard—we were collectively impressed.

The house still smelled like new carpet and fresh paint, and instead of heading straight to the kitchen for a beer as I normally did at work parties, I looked around and admired the mood lighting, live plants and furniture that matched. The producer offered to show me around, and that's when I noticed how the music followed us from room to room.

"Where's that coming from?" I asked.

"Speakers," she said, pointing at the ceiling.

Perhaps it was the speakers that did it. Ambiance. I remembered what the minister told Shawn and me after we'd taken personality tests as part of our premarital counseling. That is, after he laughed at the test results and said, "Good luck!" He said that Shawn and I were extroverts, which was the only thing about our personalities that matched. And surprisingly, Shawn was much more extroverted than I, even though he worked behind the scenes while I was on camera and in the spotlight. I scored closer to the middle, an introverted extrovert, perhaps?

"You're going to have to be clear with each other about who does what," the minister advised, still chuckling. "Who does the laundry? Who takes out the trash? And when you're searching for your first house," he said, "Angie, you'll look for ambiance. Shawn will kick the baseboards."

I already knew that Shawn was a thinker, and I was a feeler. I didn't need the minister or Myers-Briggs to tell me. I wasn't concerned. And I couldn't imagine the day when

Shawn and I would be on the house hunt, searching for ambiance and kicking baseboards. We were perfectly content living in apartments with one-year leases and no grass to cut. Settling down, buying a house and starting a family—all of that would come later. Not now, when our careers were beginning to take flight.

The Channel 5 producer's house wasn't like any of the places I'd lived growing up: apartments, townhouses, a trailer and modest one-story houses. It had high ceilings and a staircase with an upstairs landing area that overlooked the main living area. And those speakers!

Several of my good friends had gotten married and bought houses already. They spent their weekends planting flowers and painting walls. None of that had interested me, until now. Perhaps it never occurred to me that someone in the broadcast news business would settle into a space like this so early in their career. Shawn and I had been on a fast track since we graduated from college five years earlier. But I couldn't help but wonder, why hadn't we considered this? I thought about all the wedding gifts still in boxes in the storage closet at our apartment. When were we going to unpack them? And how was I going to bring this up with Shawn?

As I walked through the producer's house, I felt so comfortable. The atmosphere was inviting; it felt like a home, igniting a longing that felt brand-new and familiar all at once. A heaviness spread from the pit of my stomach into my chest—an acute sense of wanting something I couldn't have.

The childhood longings—feelings I'd pushed down in pursuit of bigger and better things—were out of the box. And there was no stuffing them back in. For the rest of the party, I chatted with my friends and sipped my beer, but as I absorbed the music pulsing through the speakers in the ceiling like a steady heartbeat, I couldn't shake the melancholy that had taken hold. It was as if I'd been transported to an earlier time, back when Mom and Cam were together, when times were good. The feeling was so close, it was like I was there. Something inside me shifted. I wanted a home. It felt urgent. Still, I wasn't ready to process what this all meant, the implications of this monumental realization.

As Shawn and I drove home from the party that night, I announced that I wanted to buy a house. He took his eyes off the road for a moment and looked at me. "Does that even make sense?" he asked. "Your agent could call with a job offer anytime."

"I know that. But who knows when that's going to happen?" I didn't have the language or a full grasp of my emotions to explain where all of this was coming from. So I said, "We're married now and we're still living like roommates." Although we slept in the same bed, we still had our personal belongings in two separate bedrooms, like we'd done when we got our first apartment together in Savannah. "I feel like we're more committed to our careers than to our marriage."

Shawn, once again, just looked at me. I knew him well enough to know that my words had stung, even if he didn't show it. Also, I knew he was processing. He heard me. And he was thinking.

Finally, he said, "Call Delaine." Delaine was my friend's mom and she was also a real estate agent. "Let's see what she says." He didn't say yes. He didn't say no. He said, let's find out more. This was so much like Shawn, never spending much time internally debating things. Unlike me, who would analyze, second-guess and turn over the situation a million times in my mind, Shawn would think. Decide. Done.

I exhaled and said, "OK."

I knew Shawn was right. Buying a house—at least right now—didn't make sense. I knew it, but I couldn't accept it. I felt a sudden, painful craving for a different kind of life with Shawn. A life filled with music and cookouts and afternoon porch sitting. A life less focused on leaving. I wanted to know what it felt like to stay.

WOUNDS

Two years after Cam adopted me, when I was 10 years old, John tried to reenter my life. My grandmother let him come to her house and see me; we sat at the kitchen counter and made small talk. I understood that our visits were a secret.

John gave me a Coca-Cola Swatch watch for my birthday. I'd been wanting one. All my friends had Swatch watches and this was one of the big ones with a rubber guard strapped across the face. I did what my grandmother advised: I told my mom that the watch was from her and my grandfather. My grandmother believed that John should be able to see me. I didn't know how I felt, about lying to my mom or about the visits. I knew that he was acting nice; he said he was sorry and heartbroken over losing me. I knew I still felt cautious around him. I knew I didn't want to hurt anybody, so I stayed quiet and went along with it.

The next thing I remember, I was sitting on my bed with my back against the pillows and the headboard. My mom sat across from me. "How dare you lie to me!" she screamed. She'd found out somehow. I fell silent, absorbing the impact. "Imagine how Cam would feel if he knew?"

Did he know? Did he question my love for him or feel betrayed? For years—decades—I would worry about that.

✦

I was 13 years old when Cam stood at the door and told me he was leaving. "I love you," he said. "I'll always be your dad. If you ever need anything, all you have to do is call."

I said OK. I didn't cry when he turned and walked out. That's what I remember the most about that moment: how I stood there, not crying. The tears were deep below the surface in a place I wouldn't be able to access for years. How long did I stand there, in the living room, staring at the door that Cam had closed behind him?

It's not like I didn't see Mom and Cam's marriage falling apart. I tried to pretend it away, escaping to my bedroom, talking on the phone to my best friend Meg, and watching episodes of "Family Ties" and "Who's the Boss?" Over the next few years, occasional fights escalated to my mom and Cam taking turns going out and coming home late. Their fights woke me up in the middle of the night. I heard the doors slam and glass break; hurtful words flew through the air, down the hall and into the bedroom where I lay still, almost frozen, until it stopped.

Years later, much later, I'd ask my mom: "Why did you get divorced?"

CHAPTER SIX

"He had a hard time showing affection," she said. "He loved me. I realize that now. He said I was making him pay for what John did to me."

After Cam left, he felt impossibly hard to reach. He remained in my life, but he pulled away just enough to make it confusing. He paid child support, but I never saw him on any regular schedule. I asked my mom about that, too. "Angie, I'm not even sure where he lived," she said. "Probably with friends."

When Cam and I did spend time together, we searched for things to talk about. The ease between us had disappeared, possibly because so many of our interactions had been felt, unspoken. I struggled to figure out ways to connect with him now that we weren't sharing the same space, navigating the routine of day-to-day life. When I looked to my mom and even Cam's mom for answers, I always got the same response: "He loves you. It's just the way he is."

My connection with Cam's parents helped me maintain my connection to him. We continued the traditions of Easter egg hunts, Christmas Eve dinners and gift exchanges. When I got older and could drive, Cam and I would sometimes meet for lunch. Even then, as we caught up on life and cracked some jokes, I wondered if he could see that I was still smitten with him. He was still my dad, and I so desperately wanted to know that I was still his girl. Sometimes I got a glimpse of reassurance when he smiled, always with his eyes.

I wanted more than him standing silently in the background. I wanted him to be a more present part of my life, but I didn't press the issue. As the years went by, I'd never understand all the reasons Cam guarded his heart. Sometimes I wondered if it was all in my head; perhaps I was just imagining it. Perhaps I expected too much, wanted too much—more than he was able to give. Love and longing became the same thing: a heart skip, a hopefulness, and then the memory of Cam walking out the door.

FOR NOW

After the party at the Channel 5 producer's house, I called the Realtor, my friend's mom. I told Delaine that Shawn and I were interested in buying a house. She said it was the perfect time, calling it a "buyer's market." Interest rates were low and property values were on the rise. Buying a house was a good investment. Shawn perked up at the word investment and now he was on board to start looking.

Before we could start, Delaine told us that we'd need to go to the bank to see how much we could borrow. It no longer felt to me like we'd succumbed to my knee-jerk reaction; it felt like we were dipping our toes in, simply testing the waters of this other completely reasonable path.

But I couldn't contain my hopeful anticipation when I got off work each day and Delaine and I spent the afternoons riding around town shopping for houses. She'd known me since I was a teenager. She was looking out for me like she would her own daughter. She understood, I sensed, that I was searching. Searching for what, exactly, I didn't know. After all the moving around I did as a child, I didn't know how to do this part. I'd never walked into a stranger's house and considered making it my own. When I moved around as a kid, I stayed with my grandparents during the transition while my mom set everything up. Mom made sure I didn't see our new home until our belongings were unpacked and my room was ready, when the place was already ours.

Delaine never seemed to be in a rush. She was content to visit every house on the list. She wanted me to see all the options and get a complete picture of what our money could buy. We did this for a couple of weeks. Finally, she said, "Have you ever thought about building?"

My first thought was no, even though I loved the producer's brand-new home, with all its speakers and ambiance. Lots of homes were being built near the television station. But the process would take months and I worried that I didn't have months to spare. As I searched for a house, my agent was still searching for my next job.

When I told Andrew we were looking for a house, I knew from the sound of his voice on the other end of the line that he raised an eyebrow. It seemed to contradict the whole purpose of having an agent. When he asked why, I should've said that I wanted to press pause and stay at Channel 5 for another year, maybe two—long enough to work through most of my contract and see how that felt. But I didn't say that because I was afraid to. I hadn't even told Shawn that. I didn't want to come off like I wasn't serious about my career, and most importantly, I didn't want to lose my agent. At that moment, I still wanted to move to Los Angeles one day. Instead, I repeated what Delaine had said to me, the words that had convinced Shawn. "Buying a house is a good investment in this market," I said. And that seemed to make sense to him, too.

✦

Shawn and I had trouble finding common ground. If I liked the kitchen, he didn't like the backyard. If Shawn liked the price, I thought the house was dirty; I couldn't unsee it. One day, Delaine and I drove by the same new construction community we'd driven past many times. "Are you sure you don't want to take a look?" she asked.

"Oh, what the heck," I said. We laughed and she turned into the neighborhood.

We learned about a house that was already under construction. The deal with the original buyer had fallen through, so the builder had dropped the price but kept the upgrades, like the screened-in porch, elongated toilets (I didn't know such a thing existed) and smooth ceilings instead of popcorn. We went to see it. There was a lot left to do. We had an artist's rendering of the floor plan, but it was hard to visualize. I tried to use my imagination.

"This house already has equity," she said, giving me a look. She was careful about not offering her opinion unless I asked, but her face said it all. This was the house. When we came back later with Shawn, he didn't need convincing. "Let's do it," he said.

We signed the contract. The process felt more like a transaction than an occasion to celebrate. It wasn't until a few weeks later, when we were out driving around on a Saturday and stopped by the lot to check on the progress, that it started to hit me that we were really doing this. We were buying a house.

We parked in the driveway and got out. We walked up the pathway to the front door, which wasn't locked, and went inside. The house had no cabinets or countertops and no flooring. The walls were Sheetrock. As we walked from room to room, finally, I could see the house taking shape. I could imagine our photos on the walls, my grandmother's table in the dining room. I could also see the blank spaces: an eat-in kitchen, two extra bedrooms and high ceilings. It would take some time to create the cozy and homey vibe that I craved, but I felt inspired to try.

We opened the sliding glass doors, entered the screened-in porch and walked out to the backyard. The sunlight reflected off the pond. We stood for a moment and watched the ducks as they crash-landed into their man-made slice of heaven. They made me laugh. I loved it all. The porch. The pond. The light.

We walked around front and Shawn took my hand as we stepped over rocks and broken bricks, avoiding muddy puddles and trying not to trip as we made our way to the edge of the dirt lot. At the street, we turned to face our home. Shawn draped his arm over my shoulder and I was flooded with deep love for him. But the flood of love also felt like an ache. A longing. A desire to stay right there in this spot and never, ever move.

"Take a picture in your mind," he said, as if he'd sensed my feelings, the words I wasn't saying. We stood there in silence, absorbing the moment. I seared it into my memory.

In a month, the house would have shutters, grass and a baby tree planted in the center of the lawn. Later, we would sit at a table in an attorney's office and Delaine would smile as we signed our names 50 million times. We would get the keys and it would be ours.

This house was not forever; it was for now. We couldn't both stay where we were and move forward. At some point we'd have to make a choice. But how could I make a choice when I wanted two things at once? How could I have these big dreams for my life and also want this?

PERFORMANCE

After Cam left, life outside of home became the balm. In the spring of my eighth grade year, the world—also known as my social life—opened up for me. I made the high school's junior varsity cheerleading team and turned my attention to the church youth group. These activities filled my time and filled me up; I felt like I was a part of something, that I belonged. That summer, Mom and I moved out of the house we'd shared with Cam into a townhouse in the same school district, at the front of the neighborhood where several of my close friends lived and a stone's throw from the railroad tracks. At night, I'd listen for the roar of the train whistle followed by the soothing hum as it blew by.

In late August, I got swept up into the fun and newfound freedom of high school: Riding to school and football games with my older friends on the cheerleading team with the windows down and music blasting, dancing in the backseat. I was also elected freshman class president, which gave my friends and me an advantage: The upperclassmen had a history of embarrassing the freshmen at the first pep rally with a call-and-response cheer they weren't supposed to know about, a minor hazing. But not on my watch. I took my job seriously, secretly teaching my classmates the cheer and telling them to spread the word. The afternoon before the first home football game when the cheerleaders turned toward our section and exclaimed, "Freshmen, Freshmen, have you heard?" I cried for joy when a hundred ninth graders responded with a roaring "yeah!" and rushed down the stadium bleachers, not stopping until they got to the bottom and almost toppled over the chain-link fence. The upperclassmen fell silent and then erupted into thunderous applause.

If I was hurting, it wasn't apparent even to me. I didn't yet understand that this outward display of vibrancy and enthusiasm was coming from the truest place—and the saddest place—inside of me. The spotlight became my solace as everything in my life that felt like home quickly fell apart.

✦

A month after I started high school, the front office secretary called the teacher over the intercom. "Please send Angie to sign out," she said. A hint of something—a concern—in her tone made me worry. I grabbed my backpack and swapped curious looks with my friends, our eyes asking the same question: Why was I going home?

As I walked down the hall, I braced myself, shaken by a sudden knowing: A few months earlier, my grandfather had had a heart attack. He recovered quickly, began daily walks and lost weight. He looked and felt good. But recently we'd learned the heart attack had done irreparable damage and he needed a heart transplant. Over the weekend, he'd been admitted to the medical university hospital to be monitored and to wait. His room was on the nicest floor in the building, with shiny hardwood floors, leather furniture and art hanging on the walls.

As I rounded the corner of the high school math wing and entered the main hallway, I saw my cousin and my mom outside the office door, in the distance. They were crying; my cousin's arms were wrapped around my mom, holding her up.

That morning, when the nurse found my grandfather on the floor of the hospital shower, it was already too late. He was gone. He was 52 years old. On the car ride from my high school back to Marilyn Drive, I sat in disbelief, sandwiched in the middle of the front bench seat, my mom's sobs ringing in my ears. When we arrived, I found my grandmother, surrounded by her sisters. Collapsed on the bed, in a fetal position, inconsolable.

In the year after my grandfather died, my grandmother sold the family home on Marilyn Drive—the place that held memories of Sunday dinners, holiday gatherings, parties in the garage and fish fries in the backyard. She pared down her possessions, bought a townhouse and went to cosmetology school to get her license to do nails.

Whenever I walked into the nail salon to visit, she greeted me with a smile and said, "Hey, Sugar." I melted at the way she looked at me, like she really saw me. Because of this, I remained in denial about the fact that my grandfather's death was the beginning of losing her too. She was never quite the same.

My mom shut down emotionally. Still reeling from her collapsed marriage and now the sudden loss of her father, she went out at night, and I buried my pain in the exuberance of football games, dancing on the sidelines to the beat of the band. My social calendar remained full: church youth group activities, hanging out with friends and dating. This is when my mom and I began to clash, when my tendency to get too serious with boys too fast became apparent. She accused me of looking for a father figure. Once, agitated by the amount of time I was spending with my current boyfriend, she asked, "Do I need to put you on the pill?"

"No!" I shouted, defensive at the accusation.

"Well, you better not get pregnant."

I wasn't having sex. I drank a few beers; I cut school once. But most of the time, I gravitated toward friends and mentors and activities that kept me grounded. Mom's assertion that I couldn't trust my own judgment in relationships, regardless of whether it was true, felt hurtful and made me feel more alone. Although I pushed back when my mom lashed out at me, I took her words to heart.

MEMPHIS

After Shawn and I moved into our new house (I kept saying it to myself: "our new house"), we mounted a flag for our college alma mater, a housewarming gift from my mom, on a column of our front porch. When I turned onto the street after work each afternoon, it was the first thing I saw, waving, welcoming, and I exhaled. It was as if the house wanted me, too, inviting me in. Coming back home was the best part of the day.

Two months later, my agent called. I picked up the phone and said hello, not giving myself time to think about what he might want. It's possible that I already knew. How could I not know?

"A news director in Memphis loves your tape," he said, voice bubbling with excitement. "She's looking for a weekend anchor and she wants to fly you out."

I sank into the couch and turned my face toward the high, smooth ceilings, searching for a response. "I don't know," I said. "I've never considered Memphis."

Countless times, I'd sat at my cubicle in the newsroom and studied the list of television news markets around the country, ranked by population. Charleston was around 100;

Los Angeles, No. 2 after New York; Miami was in the top 15. And there was the embarrassing truth of it. I'd envisioned my path unfolding just like Nancy O'Dell's: Charleston to Miami to LA. Each time I imagined getting this call from my agent, he said Miami.

I had other cities on my wish list—I wasn't trying to be completely ridiculous—but when he said Memphis, something inside me deflated. Maybe my dreams were too far-fetched. Maybe I wasn't good enough and had unrealistic expectations.

I knew I'd rolled the dice, convincing Shawn to buy a house—especially one that was still under construction, which extended the timeline even more. I knew that every month that passed inched toward this call. Now, the moment was here. I should've been more excited—I'd imagined this day many times. But the timing was terrible. "We just bought the house. We just moved in," was all I could say.

"It won't hurt to fly out there," Andrew said. "You should check it out."

I sensed that he suspected checking it out was all I needed to do to change my mind. This was only an interview. Not a job offer. I could check it out. No commitments. What would be the harm in that? How could I say no to a place I'd never seen?

"You're right," I said, agreeing once again to logic.

I had a scheduled comp day coming up, so I wouldn't

have to ask for time off. I'd fly to the interview and back and no one from Channel 5 would have to know. The Memphis station would take care of booking my flight.

I bought a new suit and a few days later boarded the plane, taking my seat in first class. I'd never flown first class and it occurred to me that this is what you do when you're trying to recruit someone. You do things like buy them a first-class ticket to show that you really want them.

That morning I put on my TV face, my TV hair and my new suit, and as the plane took off, I felt it. A sliver of excitement. Who knows? A part of me opened up to the possibility.

When the plane landed, a flight attendant pulled me aside and told me that the string that held together the slit in the back of my skirt—the one you're supposed to remove after you buy it—was still attached.

"Oh my goodness!" I laughed. "Thank you."

How, after all these years of wearing suits, did I not know about this? I felt embarrassed, but mostly, it struck me as funny. I wondered how many jackets and skirts in my closet at home had the removable strings. I hoped that Shawn, or the dry cleaners, had been taking care of that small but important detail.

I'm such a goof, I thought. I walked off the plane feeling strangely relaxed and went straight to the restroom to check my makeup, fluff my hair and remove that silly string.

The Memphis station was last place in the ratings. It didn't have the bells and whistles that came with working at a station like Channel 5: a satellite truck so you could report live almost anywhere, a helicopter and a brand-new set. But as I watched the newsroom in action and listened to the familiar buzz of police scanners, reporters making phone calls and fingers tapping on keyboards, I was reminded that no matter where you went, the job was the same. It was clear that these people were working just as hard as their competitors across town. The size of the audience didn't tell the whole story.

Amid the busyness, everyone was friendly, pausing to say hello before getting back to work. My visit felt like more of an introduction rather than an actual interview, until the news director invited me into her office. After I took a seat, the general manager popped in. He shook my hand, sat down and asked me to name three words to describe myself. I was caught off guard by this basic, unoriginal question. I couldn't believe I didn't have an answer tucked inside my suit jacket pocket, ready to pull out at a moment's notice. Why didn't I have a prepared response for a question like this? I paused and produced three basic and unoriginal answers—hardworking, dedicated, dependable—words that mean essentially the same thing.

When he left, the news director said, "I'm sorry about that. He does that to everyone." I liked her. I knew I'd get the job. And I knew, no matter what I decided, it was going to be hard. When neither option is obviously right or wrong, better or worse, how do you choose?

Flying back that night, I ordered a Bloody Mary and rested my head against the window, feeling not much different than I had before I left. It still wasn't clear to me why I was so torn. A part of me felt like it was time to move on. If I wanted to grow and advance in my career, my agent said that moving to Memphis was something I needed to do. If I stayed at Channel 5, not much would change, at least not right away. I watched the receding lights of Memphis far below and closed my eyes. It was going to take a lot to make me want to leave Charleston. It was going to take more, apparently, than my desire to be the next Nancy O'Dell. When the plane hit the tarmac, I woke up, my head against the window, the ice in my Bloody Mary melted.

I arrived home well past my 8 p.m. bedtime. Shawn was still at work and wouldn't get home until midnight. We'd grown accustomed to working opposite schedules, literally passing in the night. So I set my alarm for 3:30 a.m. as I always did and crawled into bed.

When Shawn came home for his dinner break the following evening, we finally had a moment to catch up. I rehashed the details of the interview and reiterated my mixed feelings.

Shawn said he'd become restless at work. He'd grown as much as he could in his current position as the director of the 10 p.m. newscast and he was fine with packing up and following me to Memphis. He said he'd get a job; he wasn't worried about that. Unlike me, Shawn seemed happiest outside of his comfort zone. But now, seeing how deeply conflicted I was, he said, "Don't go to Memphis for me. You have to do what's right for you."

What was right for me? This question sent me into an endless thought loop. I felt like I should want this opportunity. I wasn't completely sure why I didn't want it. I wasn't sure I could trust the uncertainty rising inside of me. Perhaps I was scared. Or perhaps, I didn't believe it was OK to say no.

GIRL

During my senior year of high school, I took an elective class, Teacher Cadets. My guidance counselor had mentioned that a college a few hours away offered one-time scholarships for incoming freshmen who'd taken the class. I thought about my favorite teachers and how I loved them. I imagined standing in a room full of students, encouraging other young girls the same way my own teachers had encouraged me. Maybe that's what I was supposed to do with my life.

I wasn't prepared for my mom's reaction when I told her. We were at Applebee's with my grandmother, having dinner after a football game.

"That's a terrible idea!" she shrieked. I was wearing my cheerleading uniform and ribbons in my hair. For the past two hours, I'd danced and shaken my pompoms for an audience of a few hundred people. But only then, as my mom spoke loudly enough for the surrounding tables to hear, did I feel like I was on display.

"You know you should be a TV news anchor," she said.

Growing up, I'd considered a lot of careers. Once, when I was still in middle school, my mom proclaimed, "You could do anything! You could write for Rolling Stone!" I think she got the idea because she'd made friends with a young attorney at her law firm who went to journalism school and had once lived in New York City. My mom's encouragement opened my mind to all sorts of possibilities—a cartoonist, for example. I'd even created a comic strip about a young woman named Zelda who looked like a cross between Cathy and Ziggy. I'd also considered becoming a young adult novelist like Judy Blume, a social worker, a psychologist, a real estate agent and an attorney.

Still, I couldn't deny that becoming a television journalist made a lot of sense; I was good at writing and public speaking and my teachers agreed with my mom. But sometimes, when I watched Nancy O'Dell anchor the news before school each day, with all her beauty and poise, the thought of pursuing a career in broadcast news felt like trying to break into show business—like the time I'd imagined becoming a child actress when I was obsessed with Alyssa Milano on "Who's the Boss?" How did people like me get on TV? How does that even work?

In Applebee's that night, it was as if Mom heard my thoughts. "You're just scared," she said.

My grandmother sat there and didn't say a word, which wasn't like her. She was my champion in all things. She was always on my side. Did she agree with Mom? I was now the age my mom was when she got pregnant with me. We were at the fork in the road, the place where I'd choose the path that would determine my future.

I pushed back. "Mom, I'd be a great teacher," I said.

"You'll hate it." This was not the first time Mom had told me how to feel about something. Like the time I told her I wanted to be a Girl Scout. "Oh, you won't like that," she said, dismissing the conversation. Or the time, just before I started high school, when I told her that I didn't want to be a cheerleader. John had made my mom quit cheerleading when they started dating, so when I said I didn't want to try out for the team, she screamed, "You're just scared!" I never found out if she was right about Girl Scouts, but she was right about cheerleading. I had been scared: worried about rumors of mean girls on the team, that I'd get a bad reputation. My experience never lived up to the negative stereotypes. Cheerleading made me come alive, and in many ways, it saved me.

Maybe she was right about being a news anchor, too. Maybe I was just scared.

I sensed that Mom was scared too, afraid that I'd turn out just like her. But what was wrong with turning out just like her? To me, Mom was strong and confident. I admired her when she left for work each day, in her high heels and hair teased up like Abby on "Knots Landing." I loved pointing her out to people—that's my mom. That night,

I understood that she was projecting, speaking from her own pain.

✦

Mom began dating a man named Patrick at the end of my junior year and things moved quickly. A month after our heated conversation at Applebee's, on a Friday night in November, they got married. I stood by my mom's side as her maid of honor.

My mom asked Chuck, the youth minister from the church, to officiate the wedding. I was glad that mom had asked him and comforted to hear that he'd agreed to do it. Days before the ceremony, he called me and asked how I felt. How did I feel about the marriage? How did I feel about the arrival of a new father figure in my life?

"I don't know," I replied.

"Well, you need to know," he said. "You need to know how you feel about it."

I was taken aback, startled by his directness, but not offended. In our weekly Wednesday night Bible studies, he challenged my friends and me. He didn't tell us what to think, asking instead, "What do YOU think?" The conversations kept us engaged and interested and he'd gained our respect and trust. A brief silence hung between us on the phone that day, and I understood that he was telling me to pay attention—pay attention to what was happening inside of my own life, inside of my own heart.

I wanted my mom to be happy. I knew that. I wondered, Am I happy? I knew how to take care of other people's feelings, but what about mine? I sensed a slight shift in awareness: I had feelings of my own, separate from everyone else's. But I'd never given them space, and I didn't yet know how.

✦

I chose the college that my high school guidance counselor had told me about, the one that gave scholarships to students who'd taken Teacher Cadets. I declared a major in elementary education and Mom didn't protest. I applied for student loans and that helped cover the rest.

During freshmen orientation, I sat in an auditorium and listened to a professor tasked with motivating and inspiring incoming freshmen. As he spoke from the podium, he explained that the next four years were the time to explore what we were interested in. He said we had the power to choose the courses we took and the power to shape our education. A curiosity rose inside me. As he spoke, a vision of my future self popped into my head. I wasn't standing in a classroom; I was sitting behind an anchor desk.

Mom said I'd been too scared to consider this path and perhaps that was true—but now, during the orientation keynote speech, I felt empowered, free to ask myself: Am I brave enough to do this? Butterflies turned in my stomach. Right there at orientation, I switched my major. The school didn't offer broadcast journalism, so I chose mass communications, the closest thing to it. I wasn't sure if this was the right path. I simply felt intrigued enough to consider it and that felt like enough.

The day I moved into the dorm, I sat on the floor of the common area pretending to listen to the residence adviser talk about whatever she was talking about. I was captivated by the pretty girls sitting next to me with the naturally curly golden-brown hair. They seemed reserved. Artsy. I was wearing an oversized sweatshirt and athletic shorts and my hair was pulled back in a headband. I looked like the cheerleader that I was, and in this brand-new environment, I felt self-conscious. I wondered if that's what they saw when they looked at me—a stereotype.

Later that night, I broke the ice. I knocked on their door, which was right next to mine. One of the artsy girls answered.

"Hi. I'm Angie," I said. "I live next door. Do you have any sharp scissors? I need to cut my bangs." I'd been growing them out all summer and I'd had enough.

"I'm Lisa. And, um, yes, I do," she said, releasing her signature laugh that I'd come to know well. "Come in."

Soon, we were sitting on the grungy carpet by the full-length mirror. We talked for hours. About our high school boyfriends. Our circle of friends. Our small towns. I'd discovered a kindred spirit. Every day after lunch, she'd come into my room and crawl into my twin bed right beside me and watch soap operas. She felt like a soul sister, like home.

There was something about the safety and security of the friendship—the genuine connection and love—that helped me see the truth more clearly: I wasn't happy there, at that school. Something was off; I didn't fit. One day, I sat on the bed in my dorm room, picked up the cordless phone and called the University of South Carolina. I asked them to send me information about their journalism program and set up a time to take a tour of the campus.

On the tour, I saw parts of the university I'd never seen before. It felt so much different than it did during those summers back in high school, during those long, hot weeks at cheerleading camp when I'd spend my days sweating on the PE fields, bunking with my team in the yucky male dorm, bathing in our swimsuits and wearing flip-flops in the community showers. When the campus tour group walked around the historic Horseshoe, I felt an energy—a connection to my surroundings—and I knew this was where I was supposed to be. I met with my adviser, filled out all the paperwork and got accepted into the School of Journalism with a focus on broadcasting. I would transfer in the fall.

This was the year that Tori Amos had released the album, "Little Earthquakes," and Lisa and her roommate made a game of it, assigning our close friends on the first floor of our residence hall a personal theme song from the album, each speaking to our individual traumas and heartbreaks. My song was "Girl," which was about a young woman who'd spent most of her life trying to be who everyone wanted her to be, rather than who she wanted to be. The piano keys evoked a haunting ache, and it was as if my friends understood there was a truer version of me below the surface of my sunny appearance. I didn't know yet who I wanted to be; I only knew that there was more that I needed to learn and discover about myself. Inside our dorm rooms, dancing together in a circle, I felt the invitation to peel back the facade and become my own person. Maybe one day.

CROSSROADS

Two days after my interview in Memphis, I met my mom for dinner at a new restaurant across the highway from Channel 5. My agent, Andrew, was on the West Coast, three hours behind us, and I kept my phone on the table waiting for his call. Mom made a huffy breath and pursed her lips before reaching over to grab a menu. I was preoccupied and she was annoyed. I ignored the passive protest and pretended to contemplate my order, but I couldn't concentrate. When the phone rang, I grabbed it and stepped outside.

"OK, here's the deal," Andrew said. "They're offering you the weekend anchor position. Fifty-three thousand dollars. That's good for the market size. And they want you for three years. Your salary will increase two grand each year."

That was $20,000 more than what I was making in Charleston! I thought about the article The Post and Courier had written about Nancy O'Dell before she left Charleston. This offer was good—it made sense for the size of the city—but a lot less sexy than Miami and six figures. I felt shame at the thought.

"Get this," Andrew said, "In a few months, the main anchor will go on maternity leave. You'll fill in for her." The opportunity to anchor evening newscasts in a top 40 market was a big deal. It would boost my credibility and look great on my resume. "And guess what?" Andrew went on. "Dayna Devon used to work there. She had the same position they're offering you. After that she went straight to 'Extra.'"

That got my attention. I watched Dayna Devon host "Extra" every afternoon while lounging on the couch weary from a long day at work. There was something about these national entertainment news shows that I loved. I hated to admit that I loved them, but they looked so fun. They were an escape from the usual topics I covered each day. I enjoyed anchoring the morning show—it wasn't all bad news; there were plenty of light-hearted moments—but so many stories felt sad and stressful to me: murders and politics, anger and controversy. My job was to be objective. Still, it was nearly impossible to not be affected.

Could I really go from Charleston to Memphis to Los Angeles? I'd told my agent that hosting an entertainment news show in LA was my dream and he was telling me once again that it was possible. I stood on a patch of grass in the restaurant parking lot as I processed the news, watching a line form out the door. I looked across the highway at Channel 5, my hometown television news station. Was my future here? Or was my future being presented to me on the other end of the line? Andrew told me to take the weekend to think about it and we'd be back in touch on Monday.

When I rejoined Mom at the table, I told her about the offer, the surprising Dayna Devon development and my frustrating internal conflict. She sipped her wine and didn't say anything, which was unlike her. It was clear she was biting her tongue, which only magnified the volume of her disapproval. I wondered if it was because she didn't want me to move away. I'd never lived more than a few hours from home, always within driving distance. Or, given the fact that Shawn and I had just bought a house, maybe the whole thing just didn't make sense to her. I didn't press the issue, because the truth was, I didn't want to add her opinions to my already conflicted feelings. So, I picked up the menu again and said, "What are you getting?"

✦

The weekend didn't bring much clarity. Shawn said he was 100 percent supportive of any choice I made, and I was grateful for that, but I also felt the weight of the decision. Regardless of his support, my decision would affect him too. I was trying to solve something that felt bigger than me and I needed some spiritual direction. On Sunday morning I asked Shawn, "How do you feel about going to church?"

"Sure," he said.

While I was growing up, there was a Bible on my grandparents' coffee table. It wasn't a real Bible—the pages didn't turn. It was more of a decorative piece, propped up on a three-legged stand. My grandmother bought it after my grandfather stopped drinking and started going to Alcoholics Anonymous. The Bible was opened to a picture of Jesus on one page and a prayer on the other: "Lord, grant me the serenity to accept the things I cannot change, courage to change the things I can, and wisdom to know the difference." I read that prayer over and over until I'd memorized it.

Back then, we rarely went to church, except on Easter when I wore frilly dresses and patent leather shoes with buckles. But Mom taught me to say my prayers before dinner and before bed every night, and when my grandmother talked to me about God, it was as if God were right there in the room. The presence was so strong, it freaked me out a little and made me feel so cold that I would shiver. "There's nothing to fear," she'd say.

Church became important to me in high school when I started going with Cam's parents on Sunday mornings. I was surprised and happy when I discovered that many of my friends from school went to that church too; it certainly made going to church seem a little less formal and a lot more fun. I became involved in the youth group and church became my second home. It was a source of stability for me, especially after Cam and my mom divorced. Going to church made me feel less alone.

I stopped going to church when I moved away to college. Without the regular connection to my friends and mentors in the youth group, church didn't feel the same anymore. I wanted to go to parties with my new college friends. I wanted to drink cheap strawberry wine. I wanted to do some things I'd never done before. I wanted to live a little. But I'd never lost interest in God. I'd always sensed a divine presence looking after me. I believed that God understood.

Now, I needed to decide about Memphis. I wondered what God wanted me to do and I hoped that the minister who married us would have something insightful to share. I prayed that his sermon that Sunday would help me make up my mind. During our premarital counseling sessions, he'd asked Shawn and me—point blank—how long we'd been living together. I almost fell out of my chair.

"Three years," Shawn replied without missing a beat.

"Has it been that long?" I asked, whipping my head toward him feigning surprise. I knew exactly how long we'd been living together. I worried that the minister would kick us out of his office, especially since we'd practically failed our personality tests.

"So why get married?" he asked.

I turned back to Shawn, genuinely curious. How did he plan to answer that? He didn't blink. "We want to stand before God, our friends and our families and make a commitment to each other."

The minister perked up, suddenly inspired, like he was having an "aha" moment. "Isn't it amazing? That after all this time, we still believe in the tradition of marriage? You could, after all, just keep living together."

"That's right," Shawn said. "We could. But we want to get married."

The minister had challenged us, but he did it in a way that made God feel accessible. God did understand. He was less concerned that we'd broken the rules and more concerned about the state of our hearts. Our actions were important, but our motives mattered just as much.

✦

Shawn and I walked down the center aisle of the church and took our seats near the front of the sanctuary. After a series of hymns and prayers (my high school youth group friends and I called all that standing up and sitting down Christian aerobics), we settled in to listen to the sermon.

The minister told us about the two brothers who had dropped their fishing nets and followed Jesus. I'd heard this one before, many times in fact. Drop nets. Follow Jesus. Got it. But something about this sermon was different. The minister stayed focused on the fishermen and the weight of their overflowing nets. He imagined aloud what they might've said: "Seriously, Jesus. We catch fish. This is who we are. Do you really expect us to drop all of this and follow you?" Their identities were tangled up in these nets, he said. The fishermen were so attached to their work they couldn't see anything else.

He closed his Bible and looked out into the faces of the congregation, "What are your nets?" He paused, giving the question a moment to land.

I wondered: What's the thing I can't live without? What's the thing I think I need to survive when it's actually the very thing weighing me down?

The minister said it again. "What are your nets? What would happen if you dropped them? What if you just let them go?"

I felt a flash of relief; for a moment I sensed what it felt like to breathe. What are my nets? The question rose within me, creating an echo. It commanded my full attention, as if the minister—and God—were both saying to me, "This is it, Angie. Answer this and you'll finally be free."

BROKEN OPEN

After my freshman year of college, I went home for the summer. Mom and her new husband, Patrick, had moved to Summerville, a town just outside of Charleston. Their house was small and charming, with a stone fireplace that made it feel cozy. Mom set up my room, like always. I was happy to be home for a couple of months and looked forward to transferring to the University of South Carolina in the fall.

Within days, it became clear that my grandmother wasn't well. Doctors said it was a bad kidney infection, and finally Mom insisted on taking her to the doctor herself. She made an appointment for first thing the following morning and my grandmother spent the night with us. Before it was time to go, my grandmother sat at my bedroom vanity, putting on makeup, visibly agitated. She spoke to our reflections in the mirror. "What are you going to do when they tell me I have cancer?" Even as she said the words, I still didn't believe that I'd ever lose her. I couldn't lose her. She was only 55 years old.

She went to the appointment and was admitted to the hospital for more tests. The next day, uncle Bobby's wife called. I answered the cordless phone hanging on the wall between the kitchen and dining room. "Hey, Angie. Is your mom there?"

"Mom's at work. She had to go in for a couple of hours. What do you know?"

She hesitated. I walked into the living room, fixing my eyes on the cozy stone fireplace.

"You have to tell me. What did the doctors say?" I pressed, pacing circles now around the open floor plan.

"Angie, it's bad."

"She has cancer?"

"It's everywhere. Her lungs. Her liver. Her brain." She started to cry. "Angie, are you OK? Are you alone? You shouldn't be alone."

It hit me like a wave. The air disappeared. "I'm OK. You need to call Mom at work. Will you? I can't do it." I had to get off the phone. She kept asking if I was OK. "Just call Mom," I said.

I slammed the phone into the receiver and fell to the floor. I buried my face in the carpet and beat the ground with my fists. No. No. No. No. I pulled the carpet with my fingers, grabbing tiny threads. I wanted to rip it up, but there was nothing to hold on to.

My grandmother refused chemotherapy but agreed to radiation. I spent nights lying by her side on the hospital bed, stroking her arm, breathing her in. Sometimes, I prayed for a miracle—instant, radical healing.

She died three weeks later, on what would have been her 38th wedding anniversary. The timing of her departure completed my grandparents' love story. I tried to find comfort in telling myself that, but platitudes didn't work. When I was driving at night, alone, I'd scream out loud. Demanding that God bring her back. There was a direct line to this grief. It wasn't complicated. It was primal, raw.

✦

After the funeral, I went back to my summer job helping in the public relations office at the South Carolina State Ports Authority. Cam worked in the engineering department and the Port offered a summer help program for employees' children. His office was in a different building, so I rarely saw him. One day, we made plans to meet for lunch.

When I got to the restaurant, the hostess greeted me and said, "Your party is waiting."

My party? I was confused, wondering what she meant as I followed her to the table. I saw the back of Cam's head. Sitting across from him was my mom. I felt caught off guard. Confused. I'd mentioned that Cam and I were having lunch that day. What was she doing here?

Cam smiled when he saw me. "Hey girl," he said in his easy, South Carolina Lowcountry drawl that made my heart skip. He stood and offered me a seat beside him in the booth.

"What's going on?"

"We wanted to do this for you," Mom said. "We wanted to let you know that we love you and you still have a family."

I was immediately transported, 8 years old again, sitting at the dinner table when we really were a family. It had never been discussed, how much I'd lost over the years. I'd felt like a bystander, watching everyone else's pain. I suspected that this meeting had been Mom's idea and I appreciated the gesture. I expressed my gratitude and maintained my poise; I tried not to get too hopeful and make the moment bigger than it was. Cam seemed completely comfortable with the plan; Mom didn't have to convince him to do this. The lunch date was easy in a way that made me feel loved and very, very sad. I held on to our hour together and carried it with me when we left. When we parted, there it was: the longing.

Back at work that afternoon, I pulled out a yellow legal pad and wrote: She was invincible to me and I watched her die. I wrote until the page was full. I ripped it out and tucked it in my purse.

✦

That fall I started my sophomore year at the University of South Carolina. I jumped right into campus life and moved into the high rise dorm with dozens of other girls in my new sorority. My grief had been so hard and heavy that summer, the instant community I found at my new college pulled back a curtain and allowed light to come in. When I walked to class each day, the campus felt alive. On weekends I went to football games and fraternity mixers. The buzz and the bigness of it all was a comforting distraction.

In the spring of my sophomore year, I enrolled in a creative nonfiction writing class that was typically reserved for juniors and seniors, but that my adviser said I was qualified to take. The professor said we could write about anything; the only requirement was that it had to be a story from our life. For the first assignment, I grabbed the yellow legal pad paper that held the words that poured out of me over the summer and went to the library. I found an open computer, typed it up and turned it in. The professor gave it back to me with her notes: "Expand here. Describe more. What did you mean here?" And that's how the class worked. We'd write. The professor would edit. And each night, I'd sit in the library, revising my drafts and feeling myself coming alive. It was as if all my life I'd been trying on different versions of myself and I'd finally found the right size—a natural, easy fit. I looked around the room, to mark the moment in time in my mind.

I wrote four essays that semester.

In one, I explored my relationship with my birth father, John. I wrote the story from John's perspective, taken from a note he'd written me in high school after he'd gotten sober and tried to make amends. He said he'd tried and now the ball was in my court. I imagined how it felt for him to lose me in the adoption. I wrote about his attempts to be part of my life in the years that followed, and how frustrating that must've been for him to be kept at an arm's length, to feel shut out.

The professor gave it back to me with a note that said, "This is a brave piece of writing. But I wonder how the story might look from your perspective?"

I was struck by the gentle way she suggested it, presenting a challenge without force. I had a voice. I had a story. And that's the one she wanted to read. It felt profound.

In the following drafts, I attempted to reconcile my relationships with John and with Cam and with my new stepfather, Patrick. In the final draft, I appeared to have come to terms with the story that I called, "My Three Dads." I'd explored the subject as much as I was capable of at the time.

At the end of the semester, I stopped by the professor's office to pick up my writing folder. Inside, I found another handwritten note that said, "You could build a career around your writing ability." Next to her signature was my final grade: A.

I would eventually learn that TV news stories called for a different style of writing—more objective and straightforward. It would take years to give my creative voice the space that it needed to return to the personal writing I did in that class, but I never forgot how it felt that day, as I walked across campus back to my dorm, clutching the writing folder to my chest. Perhaps I floated.

NETS

What, for the love of God, were my nets?

I tried to talk to Shawn about the sermon on the ride home, but it didn't have the same impact on him. He listened to me analyze it, but I needed more than that. I needed feedback.

When we got home, I grabbed the phone and plopped down in a diagonal position across the bed. I called my mom. Even though she'd acted closed off to the conversation at dinner on Friday, I knew if I asked her directly, she would tell me what she thought, because she always—eventually—told me what she thought. Now, I needed to know.

When she answered, I told her about the sermon. "The minister wanted us to identify our nets. So, I'm trying to decide: What's the heavy thing I'm carrying around that I need to drop? I'm clearly conflicted about this offer in Memphis, but I can't figure out why."

She paused. "I think your net is the desire to be famous."

Her response surprised me, and not because it felt untrue. For years she'd told me not to let fear boss me around, and since college, I'd pushed myself out of my comfort zone, again and again. I wondered why Mom suddenly seemed to be questioning my goals, or perhaps asking me to question them. I thought this was what she wanted for me.

After we hung up, I pulled out my journal. What I was seeking didn't feel like fame, not exactly, but it felt like something close to it. I'd become so attached to my career path that I wouldn't even let myself think about doing something different. And that, to me, felt like the problem. Why wouldn't I let myself imagine anything else?

✦

Andrew was eager to get me to say yes to Memphis. He worked it out so I could talk to Dayna Devon from "Extra" on the phone, which was unbelievable to me. If I'd just listen to her story about how she'd moved from a local station in Memphis to hosting a national entertainment news show in Los Angeles, I'd realize that my dreams weren't so far-fetched. They were, in fact, attainable.

So, on Monday, I stood in front of my bedroom mirror as I dialed the number with the 310 area code. Dayna picked up right away. I stared at my reflection in my bedroom mirror as we talked. I imagined her sitting in her dressing room under the glow of bright makeup lights. Her voice projected a brand of confidence I'd always admired. Would I ever be that confident? Would I ever believe in myself that much?

CHAPTER THIRTEEN

She recalled her days of working in Memphis and echoed my own observations: The station didn't have the resources that some other stations had, but the people were easy to work with and they put on a solid newscast each day.

I told her how much I liked working in Charleston and why it felt hard to leave. "I'm working at a number one station. We do have the resources and a strong team. I have a good thing here. But I want to have a job like yours one day, too."

Before we hung up, she gave me some advice: "You don't need to go to Memphis to get where I am." Immediately that felt like a permission slip to say no. "But you do need a rock star demo reel," she added.

"Angie, you DO have a rock star reel and it got you an anchor job in Memphis," Andrew said when I called him immediately afterward. "I can get you to Los Angeles, but not from Charleston. I wouldn't have brought this to you if I didn't think it was a good move." He needed an answer. He said he could negotiate for more money and other perks. "But I need to know you're really interested in this job before I do that," he said.

"I'm sorry, I can't," I finally confessed. "I believe there's something else for me out there. I don't know what it is, but I'm willing to find out."

I hung up, an internal weight lifted. And I stuck to my decision, even when Andrew called back one more time to make absolutely sure.

It's entirely possible that I was afraid to take this next step; when opportunity knocked, I choked. It's also possible that the voice within saying "you don't want this" was my own heart and soul speaking to me, telling me the truth. This doesn't feel right. Not this. Not now. The answer is no.

TRAJECTORY

During my junior year at the University of South Carolina, I enrolled in a television production class. On the first day, the professor passed out a list of student names and phone numbers. I saw a name that I recognized. Shawn Moffatt. A friend had told me about Shawn. She said that one of the journalism professors had named an editing technique after him. He called it "The Moffatt Method." According to my friend, Shawn had a reputation for not exactly doing things as the professors instructed, but he got away with it because doing things his own way worked too.

I scanned the room and my eyes landed on a cute guy with glasses and dark brown hair that was short in the back but with longish bangs, which required frequent head tossing to keep them out of his eyes. I'd seen him around campus and I put the name and the face together. It was him.

Since Shawn seemed to know more than the other students in the television production class, including me, he agreed to meet with a group of us several times, showing us how to work the camera and edit video after the professor's instruction had left us lost. I admired his cool confidence, the contrast to my nervous laugh. I was worried that he'd lose his patience, and with me in particular, but he never did. I relaxed and eventually I got it. I discovered my ability to learn by doing, and the technical aspects of broadcasting felt much less intimidating to me.

I started planning my routes so I could bump into Shawn on campus, always acting casual, as if our chance encounters had happened by accident. One night I saw him at a bar. We waved at each other from across the room, and I spent the rest of the night playing it cool, pretending not to look at him. As he was leaving, he walked over to where my friends and I were standing, touched my arm and said, "We need to go out sometime."

I smiled and said, "You have my number." I answered so quickly I surprised myself.

"Damn, girl!" he replied, equal parts shocked and impressed by my sass. But also confused.

I backpedaled and laughed. "Oh, I mean, you really do have my number. It's on the class roster. Call me!"

Shawn and I started meeting up at parties, and halfway through the semester, we went on our first date. Shawn picked me up in an old, silver Chevette with the windows rolled down because there was no air conditioner. He did not act embarrassed or apologize for this. He'd bought the car with his own money. He had a motorcycle, too, which he'd also bought himself. Like me, he got a job at the mall when he was 16 (he worked at an airbrush store and I was a hostess at Ruby Tuesday) and went to college on student loans. Since we were in the exact same financial situation, we often went to dinner at bars on half-price nights and took turns paying the tab. The more time I spent with him, the more I liked him, and by the end of the semester I was head over heels. Though it was obvious that we had opposite personalities, it didn't seem to me that, at the core, we were all that different.

During our early phone conversations, I learned that Shawn had also grown up with a lot of loss. His dad died suddenly of a heart attack when Shawn was 8 years old. It happened in the middle of the night, a few weeks before Christmas. When he and his sister woke up for school the next morning, the ambulance had already come and gone; their mom broke the devastating news. His mom remarried once and quickly divorced, and the rest of his family lived in New York state. For years, it had been just the three of them on their own.

Below the surface of Shawn's cool confidence was a gentleness that I adored. When he went home to visit his mom on the weekends, he'd call to tell me about all the snacks she'd sent back to school with him, like Fruity Pebbles and Tang. He called the treats out by name as he pulled them out of the bag.

I knew right away that he was different from other guys I'd dated. My past boyfriends had always been older than me; Shawn and I were the same age. Our friend groups intersected. We'd go to a party and immediately split up, meeting up again at the end of the night. He wasn't jealous; he had career goals and appreciated that I had my own. But sometimes, Shawn's independence triggered my deepest insecurities. Sometimes, emotionally, he felt out of reach.

One afternoon in late November, after we'd been dating for nine months, we were hanging out in my dorm room after lunch. He looked me in the eyes and for no apparent reason said, "I love you."

I stared at him, happy, relieved and dumbfounded. "I love you too, but um, why today? Why now? What took you so long?"

He said he'd held on to the words until he knew. He told me he didn't want to say it if he thought he'd ever have to take it back.

After that, I relaxed. I dropped my intense need to know: Where is this relationship going? Knowing that Shawn wasn't going anywhere was enough.

✦

Around this same time, Nancy O'Dell left her morning anchor job in Charleston to work at a television station in Miami. The Charleston newspaper, The Post and Courier, wrote an article about her huge career leap and new six-figure salary (which Nancy would neither confirm nor deny). I clipped the article during one of my weekend visits home and took it back to school with me. I'd hold Nancy's photo next to my face, staring at both of us in the mirror. I did this an embarrassing number of times, always frustrated by the disparity.

"How can I get my hair to look like that?" I asked a sorority sister as I studied my reflection. I was sporting a Pat Benatar circa 1983 love-is-a-battlefield mullet. I'd mistakenly thought the layers would make me look more professional.

"You might try Velcro rollers and a better hairdresser," she replied with a smile.

I would eventually get a better hairdresser, take lessons from the makeup artists at the MAC counter and stop buying my suits from the juniors department at Dillard's. I'd also discover an industry secret: Good lighting is everything.

After graduation, Shawn stayed in Columbia and moved back home with his mom. He wanted to go to law school and spent his days working as a runner for a law firm and his nights studying for the LSAT. I moved back home to Charleston, waiting tables at my uncle Bobby's restaurant and mailing out my resume. After a summer of going to the beach and running baskets of chicken fingers to patrons in the cocktail bar, I decided to take the advice of the journalism professors: It was time to stop leaving voicemails. It was time to just show up.

Mom took me to the mall and bought me a red suit to wear to interviews. Shawn and I spent a week in the car, traveling to TV stations in the Southeast, delivering my resume tape that highlighted the work I'd done for the campus station in college. I scheduled appointments when I could, but when I couldn't get through to the news director, I'd show up and sit in the lobby and wait until he or she was available to meet with me. Most of the time, I got the meeting. One of my professors always said, "If a news director refuses to see you and you're right there in the lobby, it's their loss. You could be the next Katie Couric." I met with several news directors that week, but I didn't leave those meetings with a sense that anything would come of it. They told me I didn't have enough experience and I wondered—how do I get experience if I can't get a job?

On the last night of our trip, I sat in a hotel room in a small town in Georgia, watching the news on the cable-access station I'd visited earlier that day. I had heard that they only paid reporters about $12,000 a year, but it was the one interview that had felt promising. The newscast was a low-budget production, and the graphics were so poor that during the five-day forecast, the weatherman might as well have been holding up a drawing of a sun with a smiley face. I watched in horror, and finally Shawn turned to me and said, "Angie, I support you in anything. But I don't support this. You can't work here."

When we returned from our road trip, I called the news director at the station in Columbia where I'd interned in college. I'd already called him several times since graduation. And each time, he told me he didn't have any reporter openings. So, I prefaced this conversation by saying, "I'm not asking for a job. I need your advice." I told him about the tiny station in the small town in Georgia, the only place that wanted me. "Do I need to take that job? Is that my only hope?"

"Angie," he said, cutting me off. "Friend to friend? Don't take that job. By the way, would you like to produce?"

I didn't know how to produce a newscast, since I'd focused my studies on learning how to be a reporter. I told him I'd learn. Suddenly, with one well-timed phone call, I had a job. My professors always said to figure out a way to get your foot in the door; that was the key to success in this business. I was in. Barely 22 and I had an entry-level salary with benefits. The beginning of an actual career.

✦

I moved back to Columbia and rented an apartment with my college roommate. Shawn was still living at home and waiting to hear whether he got accepted to law school. He called me early one Saturday morning. "I got the letter," he said, matter-of-factly. "I didn't get in."

An hour later, he picked me up and we drove to a sports bar in Five Points, and one of his fraternity brothers joined us. We drank pitchers of beer and tossed peanut shells on the floor. The following morning, he said, "It's time to start looking for a job."

We went to the television station where I worked so Shawn could put together a demo reel from the stories he'd covered in college. When we got to the newsroom, my boss was there. I knocked on his office door and popped my head in. "My boyfriend's working on his resume and needs to use the edit bay. Would that be OK?"

"Sure," he said. "Go right ahead." As I turned to walk out, he stopped me. "Can he shoot video?"

"Yes, he can," I said.

"Well, tell him to come see me." And just like that, my boss offered him a job.

Shawn worked as a news videographer on the day shift. I continued to work the night shift, coming in at 2 p.m. to produce the 11 p.m. newscast. After doing this for a few months, my boss decided to give me a shot on the air. It was the day the 1977 version of "Star Wars" was re-released in movie theaters. We were doing the whole newscast from the cinema lobby and Kathy, the main anchor, helped me figure out what to say when the camera turned to me, live. In my peripheral vision, I glimpsed myself on the TV screen, smiled a gigantic, nervous smile and started talking. I quickly ran out of air and had to pause to complete an awkward swallow. I made it through.

When we went to a commercial break, Kathy jumped up, gave me a high-five and hugged me. "You did great!" she said. "It keeps getting easier."

Kathy took on a loving-but-bossy big sister role with me, whipping me into competitive reporter shape. Her husband flew F-16s in the Air Force, so she'd worked at lots of different television stations—stations in cities much bigger than Columbia. Kathy coached me on how to make my stories more dynamic, because a good demo reel was the ticket to breaking into larger markets.

By this point, Nancy O'Dell had left the station in Miami to host "Access Hollywood" in Los Angeles. Sometimes I'd slip into a daydream: I was driving along a West Coast highway in a red convertible BMW, top down, under blue skies and a canopy of palm trees. When I imagined what my future would look and feel like, that is what I always saw: the wind in my hair, the sun shining down, and the satisfaction of knowing I'd done something big with my life. That looked like happiness to me.

✦

I had been working in Columbia for about a year when my boss got fired, which was typical in television news. It was all about the ratings and our station was in last place. He quickly found a job as the news director at a station in Savannah. As soon as he got there, Kathy called him.

"I told him that he needs to hire you, and if he doesn't make you an anchor, you're not coming."

I laughed. But she wasn't kidding.

"That's what you need, Angie. Anchor experience."

Kathy was convincing. Within the month, I was hired to be the weekend anchor. On the other days, I'd report for the afternoon newscasts.

Shawn told me to go without him. "There's not a good, professional reason for me to go to Savannah," he said. I pushed aside my hurt feelings. Savannah, Columbia and Charleston were all relatively close. What's a couple hours in the car? I told myself. We'd make it work.

I didn't have much time to contemplate the separation because shortly after I got offered the job, my boss offered Shawn a job in Savannah too. In addition to working as a videographer, he'd also train to direct newscasts. Shawn accepted the offer because the opportunity to learn a new skill was a good professional reason to go.

Shawn and I decided to rent an apartment together. I hesitated at first. I said I didn't want to play house. Our friend Allan spelled it out for us. "Guys, you're not playing house. You're broke. You need roommates."

No one could argue with this. If we each rented a one-bedroom apartment, it would break our budgets. If we were going to go through the trouble of getting roommates, in a city where we didn't know anyone yet, why not be roommates together? We found a place with two bedrooms and two bathrooms about a mile from the station. Shawn kept his stuff in his space and I kept my stuff in mine. Shawn cleaned his bathroom. I cleaned mine. We split the rent and utilities down the middle, putting two checks in the envelope. Even the grocery bill was divided fairly. I didn't pay for his razors. He didn't pay for my tampons, or the cat food. The cat had been a college graduation gift from my aunt. Shawn tolerated the cat. We were great roommates.

My first weekend newscast was a disaster. I couldn't keep up with the teleprompter and Shawn, who was still in training as a director, put a graphic over my face. But by March, we'd both hit our stride. On St. Patrick's Day, our team coverage began before dawn. I ate green grits live on the air and provided continuous reports during the city's famous parade.

One of my childhood friends, Michele, lived in Savannah now, too. She'd gone to the Savannah College of Art and Design and was launching her career as a fashion designer. One night she invited me over to her downtown apartment. She served potato leek soup and bread as jazz music played in the background. After dinner, we sat on the sofa, drank wine and petted her fluffy Himalayan cat. I'd known Michele since elementary school. We cheered together in high school and were a part of the same close-knit friend group. Michele seemed as easy-breezy now as she did back then. She was relaxed in her space. She didn't seem anxious about the future or her current station in life. Michele wore a sense of calm like the perfect pair of jeans. That night, I also noticed myself, the contrast. I felt an undercurrent of stress that I couldn't quite put my finger on, and I suspected that it was because my career path was difficult in ways that I didn't want to examine. Something felt off, but I brushed it aside. Stress, I told myself, came with the territory.

✦

Less than a year later, our college friend Mary, who now worked as a producer at Channel 5 in Charleston, called to tell me about a job opening. One of their reporters was leaving, taking a job in Miami. Miami. Just like Nancy O'Dell. It felt like a sign. All my hard work was finally paying off.

On a sunny Friday afternoon, I pulled into the Channel 5 parking lot for my interview, radio blasting and heart beating in my throat. The station had recently moved from an old building in a flood-prone area of downtown Charleston to a brand-new, top-of-the-line facility in the suburbs. They had a satellite truck and helicopter. I said a quick prayer, reminded myself to breathe and got out of the car.

I was ecstatic when I received a job offer. Going back home to Charleston to work in TV news was—literally—the beginning of a dream come true. Once again, Shawn encouraged me to go. We once again justified that we'd only be a couple of hours apart, an easy drive. I moved back in with my mom. Shawn said he'd lived in Savannah long enough to find a roommate.

But he wouldn't have to do that.

A month later, my new boss at Channel 5 called me into his office. "Hey, isn't your boyfriend a director?" he asked.

I didn't know for sure, but I guessed that Mary had put in the good word for Shawn, too. Knowing where this was headed, I tried not to jump up and down in the middle of his office. Instead, I suppressed my glee and boasted Shawn's credentials.

"Well," he said. "Tell him to give our production manager a call. We have a job for him."

This would be the last time things worked out so easily.

THE DIVIDE

After I turned down the job offer in Memphis, Andrew and I chatted a few times about other potential opportunities, but nothing came of any of them. My mom hinted that it was time to start a family—the house had two extra bedrooms after all—but I wasn't ready to be a mom. Shawn and I wanted kids—one day—but we agreed that becoming parents wasn't the immediate solution to the invisible question that hung in the air between us: What comes next? What now?

One night, Shawn dropped an industry magazine on the kitchen counter and pointed to a listing in the classifieds. "I'm going to apply for this," he said. The listing announced that "a television station in a top 20 market in a beautiful city" was seeking a technical director. It didn't say which beautiful city. It was an anonymous listing instructing applicants to send tapes and resumes to a generic P.O. box. This was common; news channels were often quiet about internal changes. They didn't like showing their hand to the competition. "What do you think?" I knew he wasn't asking for my opinion; he wanted my support.

"I think it sounds great," I said. At the time, the idea of a top 20 market in a beautiful city did sound great. Shawn mailed the tape, weeks passed, and I forgot about it.

✦

One Sunday afternoon in early May, I sat on the screened porch watching the ducks play in the pond as Shawn mowed the lawn. A familiar sadness crept up again, reminiscent of the night the producer gave me a tour of their brand-new house. I wanted more moments like this, moments when we were home together, investing in and living in our space. I thought of all those weekend nights when Mom and Cam were together. I could almost hear the vinyl records spinning on the stereo and smell the steaks cooking on the grill. I wondered why Shawn and I never did simple stuff like that. We enjoyed each other's company, but we were always moving, going, never slowing down for long. I wanted to enjoy each other, right here. At home.

I imagine I could've remedied the feeling by simply turning on some music and running to the store to buy a couple of steaks. Instead, when Shawn finished cutting the grass, I met him in the kitchen and suggested we consider staying in Charleston for a while.

"Angie, I can't," he said, in a matter-of-fact tone that stung. "I feel like we've both gone as far as we can go here. I'm not looking for a retirement job."

He stood by the sink. I raised myself up to sit on the counter. "I'm not looking for that either, but what about us? We have a great house, plenty of friends. We love Charleston."

"I'm bored. I'll go crazy if we stay." He looked directly at me, but shifted to lean against the counter, softening his stance.

"I'm not talking about settling," I said, noticing my own elevated volume, the shift in my tone. "Not the kind of settling that means being complacent. I'm talking about being content. There's a difference."

Were we only capable of being happy together when we were striving for something just beyond our reach? When would it be enough?

We agreed on one thing: We were tired of working on opposite schedules. We wanted to spend more time together, so I suggested talking to the news director to see what he could do. It was a short-term solution at best, and a misguided one. Shawn was trying to leave, and I was trying to make staying feel right.

✦

Rita had hired a new boss to run the newsroom, a young guy with a Boston accent named Don. When I had to make quick editorial decisions in the heat of the moment, Don wouldn't berate me—a communication style I'd grown accustomed to in the news business—even if he disagreed. Instead, he said things like, "Fair enough."

I was comfortable approaching Don about my desire to get on the same schedule with Shawn, and he didn't have an issue with me making the request. He said he could move me to the night shift in a couple of months, after the May ratings period. The shift change would mean I'd arrive at work at 3 p.m. and do live reports for the afternoon newscasts and the 11 p.m. newscasts. In addition, I'd anchor the 10 p.m. show, the same show that Shawn directed. It would be a lot of work, but I said I could handle it. The most important thing was that Shawn and I would be together more often.

But that wasn't going to happen. One evening a few weeks later, the phone rang. The caller ID read KOIN TV. A television station! Could it be California? It was possible because the first letter was K. All the West Coast stations started with a K.

What did they want? Why were they calling me directly instead of calling my agent? And just that quickly, I got swept up in shiny, sparkly possibilities. I picked up the phone and answered with a breezy hello.

"Hi," a woman said. "Is Shawn there?"

Shawn? That was not what I expected at all. "Um, he's at work right now. May I take a message?"

The woman on the other end of the line said she was the senior director at the CBS station in Portland, Oregon. She'd received Shawn's resume and demo tape and thought he did good work. She'd love to talk to him. Ah! The unnamed city in the ad. Portland was "the beautiful city in a top 20 market."

I stood in the middle of the kitchen for a few minutes after I hung up the phone. I didn't know what to do with myself. I was disappointed and embarrassed for assuming the call was for me. Then, I felt proud of Shawn. This was a big deal. In a matter of seconds, I went from excited to disappointed to feeling excited all over again. Maybe that was why Memphis didn't feel right. Because Shawn was supposed to get this job in Portland! And maybe Portland would have an opportunity for me, too. What if this was the call we'd both been waiting for?

I couldn't wait to tell him.

I DO

It was Shawn's 25th birthday and he suggested we celebrate at 82 Queen, a restaurant in Charleston's historic French Quarter. He'd asked me to make the reservations, which I'd suspected was all part of the act. I imagined that he'd called back later to explain his elaborate plan to propose.

When we arrived at the restaurant, I eyed the hostess, looking for any signs of conspiracy as she led us to a romantic table for two in the center of the courtyard. She acted normal. I felt a flash of disappointment when she said, "Enjoy your meal," and walked away.

Shawn pulled out my chair, as he always did, before taking his own seat. He looked handsome. His blue eyes pierced through the lenses of his glasses. He wore a navy jacket and the yellow tie my mom had given him at Christmas. I wore a little black dress I'd owned since college. We were dressed up, but not too dressed up. Just dressed up enough to keep me guessing.

When the meal arrived, I pushed my engagement fantasies aside and turned my attention back to the present. We talked about how I'd surprised him with a new surfboard earlier that day. We contemplated whether he'd get lessons or teach himself. We talked about how I would gladly support his new hobby from the safe, dry sand—far away from the sharks. The conversation flowed easily, as it usually did between us, but when the waiter cleared our plates and there was no proposal, I sank.

Still pretending to be nonchalant, I smiled and quickly excused myself. I caught up with the waiter and handed him the candles—a two and a five—that I'd hidden in my purse. "Please stick these in some type of dessert," I said. "But don't sing. He'll hate it if you sing."

I locked myself in the ladies' room and stared at my reflection in the mirror. I needed to get it together. I placed my hands on either side of my face, like I was talking to a child. "It's Shawn's birthday. Don't ruin it. You're not getting engaged tonight." Did I expect to find a diamond on the bottom of my glass of white zinfandel? Skipping over the obvious question (Why was I still drinking white zinfandel?) and answering the more pressing one: Yes. I suppose I did. I'd gotten too carried away and too hopeful. I took a breath and shook off the expectation.

I returned to the table as the waiter arrived with an ice cream sundae aglow. Shawn smiled like he knew it was coming, and the waiter walked away not singing, just as I'd instructed. I whispered the "Happy Birthday" song and told Shawn to make a wish. He closed his eyes and blew out the candles. Then he looked at me. He was fiddling with something under the table. I held my breath.

He pulled out a black velvet box. He opened it and said, "My wish is for you to be my wife."

As it turns out, Shawn really had requested that special table and he'd planned our engagement for more than a year. After radiating annoying calm all night, he now looked like he might pop. He couldn't wait to tell the story. He told me that he found the ring when we were still living and working together in Savannah, before I got the interview in Charleston.

"Oh, wow," was all I could say.

It all hit me now: When I left Savannah for the job in Charleston, Shawn had never once hinted that he was making payments on a ring. At the time, we had no way of knowing that Shawn would get a job in Charleston too. Still, he had supported me. He told me to go. He never made me feel like I had to choose between my career ambitions and him.

I'd always felt free to leave. He never seemed threatened. He never made me feel like he couldn't handle the separation. Our relationship had never been shaken by the unknown.

But I also never thought about how it would feel if the tables were turned and I was the one getting left behind.

✦

Shawn and I knew we'd need to take on the bulk of the wedding expenses. We booked our honeymoon with a credit card, and then Mom, Cam and I met one evening and agreed to split the cost of the ceremony and reception three ways. Cam had sticker shock when we went down the line items. "Times have changed," he said. But he didn't think Mom and I were being unreasonable. He wanted to host a nice wedding too.

Moments before I walked down the aisle, Cam took my arm and told me it was time. My stomach did that familiar flip-flop. He led me to Shawn and took a seat in the same row as Mom and Patrick. At the reception, we danced the father-daughter dance to Simon and Garfunkel's "Bridge Over Troubled Water." I looked around at the crowd of friends and family encircling us, sipping cocktails, ready to celebrate.

Shawn's family had flown in from New York. The night before, my uncle Bobby had invited them, along with the entire wedding party, to his house for the rehearsal dinner. He transformed his backyard into a courtyard that would rival any Charleston restaurant, telling me he did it for my grandparents as much as he did it for me. "If they were alive, they would've done this," he said. They didn't have a lot of money, but they would've found a way.

As the wedding DJ turned up the volume, inviting everyone on the dance floor to get the party started, one of my grandmother's sisters pulled me aside and embraced me with tears in her eyes, "Oh, how I wish Frances and Bobby were here. They would've been so proud."

"They are here," I said. I felt their presence, my grandmother's especially, all around.

I joined my mom on the dance floor and fell in step to the Electric Slide. I took it all in, processing how far I'd come. How far Shawn and I had come together. On my wedding day, I believed I'd taken the story of my childhood and tied it up in a pretty bow. And my new story, the one I was writing with Shawn, was just beginning.

PORTLAND

An hour after I got the phone call from the news channel in Portland, Shawn came home for his dinner break. I told him about the television station call letters that appeared on the caller ID. His eyes got wide.

"The call wasn't for me," I said. "It was for you."

Shawn returned from the interview in Portland a week later with a look on his face that told me everything. He took the job. The video he'd recorded on his trip showed a city painted with blue skies, green trees and bright sunshine. This would become our evidence to offer our East Coast Southern friends and family who'd ask, "Portland? Doesn't it rain a lot there?" Or "Where is Shawn going? Nebraska?" We'd tell them that Portland was located all the way across the country, in the Pacific Northwest, that there were apparently a few months when it didn't rain at all, and that it was undeniably beautiful.

Shawn called our Realtor, Delaine, from our bedroom telephone. As I sat on the bed and listened to him tell her the news and ask what we should do about the house, it hit me: Shawn is moving. I stared out the window into the backyard and tears rolled down my cheeks. It wasn't unlike me to cry—it doesn't take much—and he didn't act surprised when he hung up the phone and saw my red face.

"I only need a year," he said in an attempt to reassure me. "I need to get experience in a big city, but I don't care where we go after that."

He told me that since we'd only lived in the house for seven months and new houses were still going up all around us, Delaine advised us to list the house for rent instead of trying to sell it right away. When she'd said that buying the house would be a good investment, I don't think she imagined we'd be leaving so soon.

Shawn and I decided that I'd stay in Charleston until I got a job in Portland, or we found someone to rent the house. This was how we'd always done it in the past when I'd gotten a new job: Shawn would stay behind until a clear opportunity, the obvious green light, appeared. Why would it be any different this time? Was there any reason to believe it wouldn't all work out?

✦

When Shawn walked into Don's office to turn in his resignation, Don said, "You're a rat bastard." Then he said, "Congratulations." After the meeting, Shawn passed my desk and told me it was OK to go in next.

"Knock-knock," I said, announcing my arrival and easing into the chair across from Don.

"I told your husband he's a rat bastard," he replied.

"I heard," I said, laughing.

"Nah, really, he'll do great out there. We just hate to lose him."

"I know," I said, pausing for a moment, feeling the weight of it—the reality of Shawn leaving—once again. "I just wanted you to know, this came as a surprise. Everything happened at the same time ..." I trailed off. What was I doing? Making excuses? Apologizing? A little of both. I'd asked Don to move me to the night shift so Shawn and I could be on the same schedule, and now Shawn was leaving. By trying to fix it, I'd made it worse. Staying on the morning show wasn't an option anymore because my replacement had already been selected. I wished I'd left it alone. "I'm not going with Shawn right away, but I don't know what's going to happen. If you change your mind about moving me to the 10 o'clock show, I understand."

"No," Don said, shaking his head. He understood what it was like trying to navigate a relationship in the transient business of television news. Once, his girlfriend, Stephanie, worked in Medford, Oregon, while Don worked six hours away in San Francisco. "I know you'll do your job and do it well as long as you're here. We'll stick with the plan."

Stick with the plan. He made it sound so clear and simple. Even then, I was still trying to pretend that Channel 5 offering me the three-year contract, buying the house and saying no to Memphis hadn't thrown my whole world—everything I thought I wanted—out of orbit. Stick with the plan. That was the one thing I couldn't do.

✦

When Shawn moved to Portland, I imagined that he would get an apartment. I imagined that we'd figure out a way to fly back and forth across the country to see one another. I imagined that it would be hard, but we'd figure it out. I never imagined that Shawn would get a roommate. But during the interview in Portland, Shawn had learned that the station also needed a graphics operator and suggested they call our co-worker, Chris. As Shawn predicted, the Portland station loved Chris, and they hired him, too. Suddenly, they were whipping up a plan to share an apartment.

I liked Chris. He struck me as the kind of guy who would put down the toilet seat and wipe the spit off the bathroom mirror. And yet, I was furious with Shawn, and hurt. How could he get a roommate? We were closer to 30 than 20 now. Full-fledged adults. This felt like a plan college people came up with. Like single people came up with. Did married people do this? How exactly was renting a two-bedroom apartment with a young, single guy the same as waiting for your wife to arrive? I'd wanted Shawn to find an apartment for us. I tried to explain this to Shawn, but he dismissed my concerns. I could tell he thought I was overreacting.

"It's only a six-month lease," Shawn explained. "If you move to Portland before the lease is up, we can all live together. Chris is good with it."

"Well, that's very nice of Chris. But I'm not good with it."

"Angie, we still have this mortgage, so it will save us some money, and Chris and I can get a better apartment together than we could on our own."

It all made sense. I got it. I still didn't like it. I felt left out, but I sensed that I wasn't being completely fair. I didn't want to fight about it anymore, so I let it go.

The night before Shawn left for Portland in early August, we sat on the floor eating takeout and watching a movie. I had to get up and leave the room, pretending I was going to the bathroom, because I was choking back tears I didn't want him to see.

Shawn had always supported me. Anytime I'd ever wanted something—the move to Savannah and then to Charleston—he said do it. I told him I wanted a house, he said OK. And now, I wanted him to stay, but I knew I couldn't ask that of him. It wasn't simply his turn to go; it was his time.

I tried to hide my despair. If he detected it, he was too forward focused to let it in. The next morning, he packed the car and kissed me goodbye. I stood on the sidewalk and watched him drive away. Barefoot in my pajamas, I turned to face our home. The front porch flag waved in the breeze and it welcomed me in. I loved that house—or perhaps the idea of it—enough for the both of us. I took another picture in my mind, tiptoed across the damp grass and went inside.

PART TWO

PRESSURE

It seemed that the hardest days had been the ones leading up to Shawn's departure, and now that it was done, a calm washed over me. I adjusted to my new routine. Reporting and anchoring for the evening news was a notably different experience than anchoring the morning show, when I'd arrive at the station in the middle of the night to an almost-empty parking lot and a few barely awake co-workers sipping coffee and staring at computer screens like zombies. At 4 a.m., even the police scanners were quiet. Fast-forward 11 hours, and walking into the newsroom was like jumping onto a moving treadmill: reporters talking on the phone, computer keyboards clicking, producers shouting across the room. And yet, on the day Shawn left for Portland, the buzzing room seemed to freeze for a moment when I entered. My co-workers greeted me with concerned faces and the same question: "How are you doing?" I told them I was fine, and I was, at least in that moment, telling the truth.

I tried to take things day by day. Delaine posted the "for rent" sign in the front yard. I parked in the middle of the garage. I checked out the fancy, brand-new health food supermarket across town and bought things that were quick and easy to prepare, like turkey hot dogs on sprouted grain buns. At night after work, I took a bath and crawled into bed, enjoying the late-night TV show lineup and falling asleep without setting an alarm. When I woke up, the sun was shining, and I laced up my sneakers and went outside. I'd never been much of a runner, but I enjoyed intervals, so I kept an eye on my watch and adjusted my pace, sprinting toward the stop sign and slowing back down to walk. I'd pretend that the stop sign was Portland—just a few more steps and I'm there—and the game made me run faster.

Why didn't I go? Why did I let Shawn leave without me? I knew the reason. For TV journalists, on-air positions were limited and competition was fierce. It felt too risky to leave my job without another one lined up, and I wasn't sure if I even wanted a job in Portland. "I only need a year," Shawn told me. Maybe after the year was up, he'd want to come back to Charleston. Or maybe, we'd go somewhere new, together. Each morning, I'd sprint toward the stop sign. The stop sign was my prayer for an answer, clear direction.

While making daily beat calls to police departments or out covering a news story and conducting interviews, I'd inevitably hear the question: "Why aren't you on the morning show anymore?" I was powerless to control public perception of what was going on behind the scenes in my personal and professional life. I was bothered by this and bothered by the fact that I was bothered, that I cared so much about what other people thought.

Some days, in the hours before work, I'd browse the aisles of the bookstore, always landing in the spiritual and self-help sections. I felt myself turning inward; the minister's question, "What are your nets?" repeated itself in the back of my mind. I still didn't know.

The one thing I did know: I loved all this newfound time I had—the daylight—before reporting to work. After my morning runs, I sat on the screened porch overlooking the pond and read for a bit. Then, I wrote in my journal. I didn't have to teach myself how to do this part, how to spend time by myself. As a child, I was completely content to spend time alone in my bedroom, sitting on the floor beside my Holly Hobbie canopy bed that matched the curtains. Mom would set the scene, surrounding me with toys and saying, "Let's pretend," and she'd quietly slip out. I chatted with my imaginary friend Melinda and listened to storybooks on the record player. I studied the pictures while the narrator read the story aloud. I waited for the sound of the chimes before I'd turn the page.

✦

One morning, a couple of weeks after Shawn left, Mom called me. With a particularly upbeat tone, she asked, "When you move to Portland, what would you think if I moved there too?"

So many legitimate concerns about why this might be a bad idea never came up that day. One was that Mom had never really traveled, anywhere. Second, she'd said WHEN I moved to Portland. At that point I wasn't clear IF I'd move to Portland. The third and most important concern, which we only discussed briefly: Mom was married.

"What about Patrick?" I asked.

When I was in college, they tried to have a baby. There was a moment when I, too, got excited about the idea of becoming someone's 19-year-old big sister. After a couple of miscarriages and a second ectopic pregnancy that sent Mom to the emergency room, she agreed to a surgical procedure that ended her chances of getting pregnant again. Patrick felt shut out of that conversation; Mom said it was her body and her choice to make.

I'd had my own issues with Patrick in the beginning. They got married so quickly, and I resented him for trying to parent me and tell me what to do. Once, he hid my car keys because I never hung them on the key rack, instead tossing them on the first available flat surface. When he finally gave them back, I stormed out and drove off without telling Mom where I was going. But that was years ago, and over time we'd moved on to a relationship that felt more cordial.

Now she was telling me that things weren't going well between them, and she needed the separation. She didn't say divorce, but as she sat at her computer at work, talking and clicking, admiring images of Portland on the internet, she also didn't mention any plans to reunite. "It's beautiful! The trees are so green. Did you know they call it the City of Roses?" She rattled on and on, listing the selling points. She was already looking at job listings at Portland law firms. I couldn't recall a time that she sounded so excited. So hopeful.

It seemed irrelevant that my commitment to moving to Portland was half-hearted at best. I didn't stop to question whether Mom was truly ready to leave her marriage, and I didn't reflect on how I felt about Patrick no longer being in our lives. At her suggestion that we move to Portland—together—I was relieved. Suddenly, I felt free to leave. Mom's bright idea to move to Portland made total sense.

I replied, "That sounds like a great idea."

After we hung up, I called Shawn. "If I move to Portland, Mom wants to come, too. What do you think?"

"That's fine with me," Shawn said. "As long as she's coming on her own terms."

"She'd get her own place and is already looking for jobs," I said.

"Great. Tell her to go for it," he said.

It was really that easy. Mom and Shawn had always gotten along and he didn't seem a bit concerned. With Chris there too, Shawn's attitude about Portland was "the more the merrier."

And it wasn't lost on me that Shawn's voice was different. He sounded happy.

Things happened quickly after that. Mom told Patrick she wanted to separate, and the following weekend she moved in with me, filling the empty garage with boxes and replacing the plastic table and chairs on the screened porch with real, grown-up-looking patio furniture: a wicker couch with cushions, matching side chairs, a coffee table. And plants. Indoor plants, outdoor plants, everywhere there were plants. Mom's stuff filled the open, echoing spaces of the house in a way that made it feel perfectly lived-in and homey. The transformation reminded me of the night I toured the producer's house a year ago, the moment that set me on this journey. I finally had the ambiance that I craved, but Shawn wasn't here, and our future felt more uncertain than ever.

Mom befriended the single, male neighbor who lived next door. I never got the sense that anything was going on romantically between them, but sometimes when I'd come home for a dinner break, I'd find them sitting on the screened porch listening to John Mayer. It seemed like the sort of fun and relaxing thing that neighbors do. I felt myself not wanting to go back to work, wanting instead to stay. The lyrics about "living it right" following me out the door.

"The house looks pretty amazing since Mom moved in," I told Shawn on the phone one day.

"It sounds like I'm missing out," he replied, with a hint of nostalgia in his voice. We talked about how the neighborhood had changed in the short time since he left. More newly built homes lined the once empty street and the community pool—which was in walking distance from our house—was almost complete. I couldn't stop imagining what life might've been like if Shawn had stayed.

We'd been apart for about a month, and I didn't know what I wished for anymore. Did I want Delaine to call with the news that she'd found someone to rent the house? Did I want Andrew to call with a new and exciting job offer in Portland? Did I want to bide my time while Shawn lived out his year there? I'd considered all these scenarios. I kept moving the pieces around in my mind, praying for the moment, the phone call, the miracle, when something, finally, would snap together.

Mom, on the other hand, had grown impatient. She was ready to go. She was ready to quit her job in Charleston and begin a new life in Portland. I felt pressured to decide.

ROOFTOPS

Mom scheduled some interviews and the following Friday we took the day off and flew to Portland. She held her breath and gripped the armrests when the plane took off and gasped out loud with each bump of turbulence. When the flight attendants made their way down the aisles, we distracted ourselves with a cocktail and the in-flight movie: "My Big Fat Greek Wedding."

We reversed roles when the plane landed in Portland. Now, I was less sure of myself; Andrew had sent my resume and demo reel to the four main television stations, but no one had responded. Mom, however, was on a mission. Shawn picked us up from the airport and we drove straight downtown so she could make her afternoon interviews. We dropped her off on the sidewalk outside the law firm and told her to call when she was done.

I felt first date jitters getting the grand tour of Portland from Shawn, whom I hadn't seen in weeks. The sun peeked through the clouds and the city seemed alive, vibrating with afternoon traffic, pedestrians and cyclists. There was a spark between us; the electricity felt reminiscent of our college days when our relationship was new.

Shawn and Chris' new bachelor pad on the 10th floor of the high-rise apartment building boasted a panoramic view of the city. Chris was at work, so we had the place to ourselves. Tall windows lining the walls opened like little doors, allowing a light breeze to flow in. Shawn loaded our favorite CDs and hit shuffle. As "Closing Time" by Semisonic played in the background, he popped the caps off two bottles of Hefeweizen, a beer Don had told us about, and pushed a lemon wedge inside each of them.

"Here you go," he said, handing me a bottle. "Do you want to go up?"

"Absolutely," I said. Drinking beers on rooftops was one of my favorite things to do.

We rode the elevator to the top floor, walked up a flight of stairs and stepped out to the patio garden. The building stood on a hill on the Southwest part of town, one block from Burnside and the trendy Northwest neighborhood. I could see Mount Hood in the distance. This wasn't the rainy forecast family and friends had warned us about. We were in the middle of a gorgeous Portland summer.

Since my career had taken off, I'd been living in a pressure cooker of long hours, loud newsrooms and intense scrutiny. That afternoon, overlooking the city and my life, I felt lighter and filled with a sense of peace. Another invisible weight lifted. An exhale.

I thought about what I'd be doing at that exact moment if I were back in Charleston, three time zones away. It would be time to report for the night shift, time to step back onto the moving treadmill of my career. On the roof, it all seemed so unimportant. It occurred to me: Perhaps it's OK to take a break. Perhaps a break is what I need.

On the roof, the only thing that felt important was that exact moment. Shawn wrapped his arm around me, resting his hand gently on my shoulder. I inhaled the freedom; it felt right to not be anywhere else but there on that rooftop. I took another picture in my mind. This moment. I wanted this too.

✦

That night, Shawn, Mom and I had dinner at an Italian restaurant on the southwest side of the city, choosing a table outside on the sidewalk patio under a big umbrella. We watched people walk by and chatted with the waitress. She told us she'd lived in South Carolina once and how much she loved Portland. Mom and I asked her about the rain.

"It rains a lot, but it's not pouring rain like you get in the south. Here, it's a misty rain, like your skin is being moisturized." We laughed at that. She added, "And the summers here are amazing."

I couldn't disagree with that. It was as if we were sitting in a photograph, with blue skies and green trees, just like those images Mom saw on the internet. As we continued to enjoy our dinner outside in the mild night air, Mom's excitement about Portland had become my own. But I didn't say anything, not then. Sunday morning, I kissed Shawn and got back on the plane as quickly as I'd arrived. We still had a mortgage. I still didn't have any job offers waiting for me. I didn't have the green light to go.

But did I need a green light? And from whom? Who needed to give me permission to join my husband 3,000 miles across the country? This move was not like the others—when I'd led the way. It was true, I'd taken those opportunities in Savannah and Charleston not knowing when Shawn and I would be reunited, but we were never more than two hours away and we weren't yet married. The stakes were arguably lower. Now, I couldn't just hop in the car and get to Portland before lunchtime. Driving to Portland would take days. We were about as far away from each other as we could get and still be in the same country.

What, exactly, were we thinking? Once again, it felt like we were putting our careers before our marriage.

When the plane landed back in Charleston, I realized that Shawn was the green light I'd been waiting for. The metaphorical sign I'd been sprinting toward on my runs each morning. Why, after the powerful moment on the roof, had

I not said anything about how I was feeling? And why had Shawn not asked me to stay? Perhaps we'd been supportive to a fault. Or stubborn.

Finally, on the phone a few nights later, I asked, "Shawn, what do you want?"

"Angie, I want you out here. I want you here now," he answered, like I'd forced a confession. Perhaps I did. But I needed to hear him say it. I wanted to know that he wanted it too.

The next day, I called Delaine. I asked her to put the house on the market. I told her that we were no longer interested in trying to rent the house to someone else. It felt less messy to let it go. Clean slate. We hadn't owned it long enough to sell it for a profit, but Delaine said she'd find a buyer quickly, and we could at least get back our initial investment.

Later at work, I went to Don's office and handed him my regretful letter of resignation, thanking him and the Channel 5 team for all they'd done for me. I gave him a month's notice.

I never imagined it was how I'd say goodbye, so abruptly and without a big career advancement waiting in the wings. As part of the Live 5 News Team, I'd helped viewers start their days with news, weather, traffic and cheery banter with my co-anchors. I'd covered history-making moments: the day the Confederate battle flag was lowered from the State House dome, when the lost Hunley submarine was raised from the ocean floor, and when the terrorist attacks on

September 11 brought the country—and our newsroom—together in a way I'd never experienced. I'd grown up on those airwaves and recovered from embarrassing moments—like the time I reported on a forest fire and said live on the air, "The fire is contained but we're not out of the woods yet," while I was standing in the woods. It took months to live that down. But over the years, I'd become a journalist who was trained to be tough, had developed a thicker skin and produced stories that were accurate and fair. On one hand, my departure felt premature. On the other hand, it felt necessary and non-negotiable.

Don asked if I'd consider staying an additional month, through the November ratings period. I told him that I was sorry, but I couldn't. I felt bad about that, but Mom was more than ready—she had a new job waiting for her—and now I was ready too. I couldn't delay this move another second.

The Post and Courier wrote about my upcoming departure in its weekly media news column, saying that I was following my husband to Portland—no mention of Miami and six-figures, as I'd fantasized about since college. Days later, I found myself typing "Meg Ryan" and "You've Got Mail" and "hairstyle" into the search bar of my computer at work. I didn't have the patience to wait until after my last day at Channel 5 to chop off my hair. I wanted to feel liberated. All that hair was suddenly too much. It weighed me down. I also removed my belly button ring that I'd gotten a year earlier, which had been secretly inspired by watching too many Britney Spears music videos on MTV. Blonde helmet hair and sparkly belly rings didn't seem to fit this new life I was headed toward in the Pacific Northwest. I felt the urge to get closer to who I really was underneath all the makeup and the lights, away from a job that required you to present the most polished version of yourself.

✦

A few weeks later, on my 28th birthday, I flew to Portland again—this time without Mom. Andrew had made some calls and arranged a meeting at Shawn's station, and I spent an hour in the news director's office, selling my experience and sharing what I loved about Portland so far. I felt particularly Southern and wondered if all those years I'd spent toning down my accent were failing me. Although I did feel good about my new Meg Ryan hair.

The news director said he'd keep me in mind if any positions came open, but he didn't know when that would be. Sometime in the new year, maybe. I liked that idea, moving to Portland and having some time to get settled before diving back into the fast-paced TV news life.

That night, Shawn and I went to Portland City Grill, a restaurant on the top floor of a high-rise bank building. We sat at a table by the window, the lights twinkling on the hillsides around us. After our romantic dinner overlooking Portland, Shawn and I moved to a cocktail table by the bar and listened to a man play the piano. The moody atmosphere and the city lights in the background felt right for this new beginning. I told myself it would be nice to take a break from TV. I needed a break. I even contemplated getting a part-time job somewhere—at a bookstore or coffee shop, perhaps, while I waited for Shawn's station to call and offer me a job. There were so many possibilities.

✦

On my last day at Channel 5, I stopped by Rita's office. As I took a seat across from her at her desk, I thought back to the day she offered me the three-year contract. Her invitation had made me feel so appreciated, so welcomed, and I wondered if she knew how much it complicated my clear-cut plan. Would she ever understand how it turned me upside down and how difficult it was to say goodbye now? How could this huge decision feel so right one minute and so completely wrong the next?

Sitting in Rita's office, I realized I couldn't reverse this choice. I couldn't bring Shawn back, unpack the house and get my job back on the morning show. I started to cry. I couldn't help it. "I just don't know if I've done the right thing," I confessed.

When I stood up to leave, Rita walked me to the door. Then she stopped and gave me hug. She looked at me with compassion and said, "Angie, you're a smart woman." She lifted her finger gently and she pointed at my chest, as if she were tapping me with a magic wand. "Trust your heart. It will tell you what to do."

ROAD LESS TRAVELED

That evening, I anchored my final 10 p.m. newscast, which ended with a surprise montage of photos of me as a child while the meteorologist and sports anchor offered play-by-play commentary. Don had called my mom and she dug through old photo albums and—thank goodness—pulled the cute ones, sparing the different variations of a mullet I'd sported over the years.

By this point in the day, I was detached from what was happening, like I was outside my body watching the scene unfold. When I walked off the set and back to my desk, I opened my email and found a note from Don.

"I know from experience that these moments can feel anticlimactic," he wrote. "But we thank you for your time here. You will be missed."

An hour later, Don and his girlfriend, Stephanie, met up at a bar with a few of us from the night shift and had a beer. Although we exchanged more hugs and goodbyes, it felt like any other night. Anticlimactic seemed about right.

✦

A couple of weeks before we left for Portland, Cam had casually suggested that he and his brother might be able to help Mom and me move across the country. Cam would drive the moving truck, his brother would drive Mom's car and Mom and I would ride together in my car. He must've thought better of it, because as our departure date got closer, he made up a reason about why he wouldn't be able to go. I didn't dwell on my disappointment. I only halfway believed it would happen anyway.

It left us with a logistical situation that Mom and I hadn't thought all the way through. Shawn and Chris wouldn't be able to take time off work to help us move. We decided that Mom would drive her car, and I would drive the moving truck and tow my car behind it.

Patrick gave Mom a pair of walkie-talkies so we could communicate on the road. He'd sounded sad when I called him to tell him goodbye. After we hung up, I wrote in my journal about the sadness that I felt too. He'd been so kind, even though Mom was leaving him.

On moving day, Cam did show up to help us load, along with my uncle Bobby and the next-door neighbor. We had a lot of stuff. Even though I'd sold the washer and dryer and living room furniture, we still had dozens of Mom's boxes in the garage. In hindsight, we needed a large moving truck, not the medium-sized one, but we agreed the medium truck was the safer option for me to drive, especially since my car would be hooked to the back.

When the moving truck was stuffed to capacity and boxes were still sitting on the front lawn, we made a last-minute decision to rent a small cargo trailer and hook it to the back of Mom's car. We had no other choice. This was the exact moment when Mom began to unravel. The thought of driving her car alone cross-country had made her nervous; being forced to haul an additional load sent her over the emotional edge.

I, for whatever reason, wasn't nervous. Stephanie had given me her best road trip tips, taking me to Walmart to buy a soft case to hold my CDs and a small Igloo cooler for snacks. My music was ready and my cooler was packed with Diet Cokes and chocolate-flavored meal replacement drinks. My cat meowed in the carrier occupying the passenger seat. I adjusted the driver's seat and the steering wheel and tossed in a pillow to sit on to give me an extra boost. It was time to get out of limbo. I was ready to go.

But first, I walked through the empty house one last time, recording it all on video, my voice cracking as I said goodbye to each room. I held on to every echo, every glimpse. I said a final, "Goodbye, house," and closed the door behind me.

I walked to the sidewalk and stood by the moving truck. My mind's eye flashed back to the day Shawn and I stood at the very same spot when it was still a construction site. I snapped another picture in my mind. I knew this day would come. I hoisted myself up to the driver's seat and turned on the ignition. I grabbed the walkie-talkie.

"Ready?" I called to Mom.

"Ready," she said. She wasn't ready. She was terrified.

I eased onto the gas and we drove our funky parade out of the neighborhood.

✦

On the road, my heart was numb; my fingers wrapped tightly around the steering wheel. I replayed the string of farewell parties, the packing of boxes and the final goodbye to the empty house. My emotions moved through me as quickly as the scenery on the other side of the glass.

I was wearing jeans, a 49ers sweatshirt and no makeup. My hair was a mess—flipping in all directions because it was now too short to twist into a clip.

My carefully selected road trip soundtrack highlighted the themes of authenticity and liberation. Christina Aguilera's "Stripped" and India Arie's "Voyage to India" played over and over. Alone on the road, I didn't feel alone at all. I was coming undone, but as long as the wheels on the moving truck were turning and the music was playing, coming undone felt right.

"Angie, slow down!" my mom's agitated voice crackled through the speakers of the walkie-talkie, interrupting my personal awakening.

Before leaving Charleston, we'd plotted our course on the map. Take Interstate 40 all the way to California. Head north on Interstate 5 until we got to Oregon. This route promised the best weather and looked like the safest way to go. But it wasn't necessarily the quickest route. I was hoping to get to Portland by the end of the week, on Shawn and Chris' day off, so they could help us unload. I was on a bit of a time schedule, but I didn't feel like I was speeding.

"Mom, I'm going with the flow of traffic," I said, trying, unsuccessfully, to tone down the bratty teenager in my voice. I checked the rearview. Traffic was heavy and she trailed a few cars behind me. I eased up on the gas and watched the speedometer decelerate. Apparently, at some point, I sped back up.

"Angie, I said slow down!"

After practically shoving me out the door, pushing me to hurry up and make up my mind about moving to Portland, her sudden desire to slow down felt ironic and annoying. I checked the rear view and this time Mom was out of sight. "Where are you?" I asked. "Do you see me?"

"You're going too fast! Your car is bouncing all over the highway."

My mom and I had romanticized our cross-country drive. We'd rented the movie "Thelma and Louise" for inspiration. We overlooked the fact that these two best friends traveled top-down in a 1966 Thunderbird. We imagined how fun it would be for the two of us to breeze along the open road together. We didn't discuss that we'd be driving separately, or the movie's ending—when Thelma and Louise drove off the side of a cliff.

Still, I identified with the spirit of Thelma and Louise's journey toward freedom. I didn't want to slow down. I wanted to drive. I needed to keep going.

✦

Since we got a late start on the first day of our trip, Mom and I drove for two hours before stopping in Columbia for the night. The next morning, we got up, grabbed coffee and rolled out. Now, as dusk fell at the end of day two, we checked into a hotel near Nashville. We hauled our suitcases inside and I plunked down on the double bed and unfolded the map. The accordion of paper seemed to play a dismal tune as I spread the United States out in front of me. I found a pencil in the nightstand and drew a line from Charleston to the Tennessee border. I used my thumb and index finger to measure the distance and started drawing lines across the map, trying—rather inaccurately—to guess how far we'd get each day.

"Mom, we have to cover more ground tomorrow," I said.

She shot me a look but said nothing. She seemed to not be concerned about getting to Portland on a day that Shawn and Chris could help us unpack. This frustrated me, and, in the hotel room that night, I noticed sitting still frustrated me too. When I sat still, the homesickness felt crushing. I tried to explain this to her. I told her I felt sad. The look on her face sent the message that I needed to stop talking. But didn't she feel it too—the pros and cons layered on top of each other? I was seeking validation, or a few words of comfort. A simple "everything will be OK." Perhaps she couldn't offer that because my doubts were pressing uncomfortably against her own.

I reached into my purse and pulled out a letter from my childhood best friend, Meg. She'd handed it to me a few weeks ago at one of my going-away parties, and I'd saved it as instructed. Meg and I had been swapping letters and analyzing life since fifth grade. We saw each other at school each day and talked on the phone every night—a welcome distraction from the icy silence followed by explosive outbursts between Mom and Cam. But handwritten prose was how we shared our innermost thoughts and feelings about life, love, loss and coming of age. We folded our secret notes, which consisted of multiple pages front and back, into compact rectangles with a pull tab to open.

Meg's most recent letter was sealed in an actual envelope with the words "to be read somewhere between South Carolina and Oregon" written in cursive on the front. I opened it and pulled out the neatly folded pages of flowery lavender stationery. It read:

"It's letter time once again. The pressure is on to say something profound and inspirational. But the more I think about your big move and the 'right' thing to say as a send-off, the more I realize that there is no right thing, no right path to take in life, no right way to feel about any chosen decision.

"Moving to Portland just is. It's only right because it's happening.

"Remember that poem every English teacher makes junior high kids read, Robert Frost's 'The Road Not Taken'? There's that famous line that teachers use to encourage students' individuality/originality:

'Two roads diverged in a wood, and I—

I took the one less traveled by,

And that has made all the difference.'

"This line leads people to believe that there was one right path, that it was the more unique, more hidden of the two paths and that Robert Frost found it, made the right decision, etc. But this isn't really what Frost is saying at all. It only 'made all the difference' because that's the one he chose.

The whole poem is really about his sadness over the fact that he couldn't travel both roads and 'be the same traveler.'"

I paused and looked over at Mom, under the covers in the bed next to me, watching TV. Meg understood where I was coming from. Why couldn't Mom? But Meg had always been my partner in analyzing deep thoughts and heavy matters of the heart. We'd offered free therapy to one another since we were teenagers, as we sat on her bed in her room with purple walls and dissected lyrics to tracks by The Smiths or lounged on Folly Beach as Sinead O'Connor breathed from the speakers of the portable boombox. Meg wasn't afraid to stare down the angst. Together, we went right into it.

I didn't understand, until Meg was enlightening me now, that not everyone saw the world the way I did. That would explain why, as someone who seemed comfortable in the spotlight—me, the popular high school cheerleader—I often felt like a misfit.

Her letter continued:

"The real problem for you is that you are a deeply feeling person who can't help but feel the complexities and layers of everything this move means. Most people resign themselves more quickly to what's 'right' or 'wrong.' For whatever reason, you are not this type of person. You can be on one path and feel the nostalgic echo of another road you decided not to take.

"This is both a curse and a blessing.

"It makes living in the here and now and embracing the present tense moment more difficult. But it also makes you wiser. You can see beyond this moment, this decision, this road. You see a bird's-eye view of your life. You can make all kinds of connections between past and present. You can draw meaning and metaphor from your gift of perspective.

"It's not about the destination or the arrival. It's about the traveling itself. Wherever you are on the journey is the 'right' place to be. Remember—you carry so much love and light and wisdom with you. You have everything you need."

I folded up the letter and stuck it in my suitcase. I went to bed, feeling hopeful about the light of a new day, when I could be the traveler once again.

✦

The next morning, after Mom and I filled up her car and the moving truck with gas, I ran inside the convenience store to grab a coffee, and we were back on the road again. A few hours into the drive, the interstate guided us around the outside of a city, buildings rising on our left.

"Hey, Mom?" I called through the radio.

"Yeah?" I could tell she was concentrating. Ten and two.

"There's Memphis."

She didn't say anything, but I felt her response. A shared

silence as we looked out our driver's side windows. I also felt a twinge of something, a wistfulness and a curiosity about how things would've turned out if I'd only said yes to that job offer. Shawn and I had a plan, born of my own professional dreams but one that we had imagined together. He said he'd support me, that he was willing to follow me all around the country if needed. But our perfect plan held opportunities for him too. We'd move up the proverbial ladder of success together.

Then I'd had a change of heart. I secretly wished that our life in Charleston would be enough. But it wasn't enough for Shawn, and if I was completely honest with myself, I was not sure that our life in Charleston was enough for me either. Even after we bought the house, as much as I wanted to stay, part of me never stopped wondering what was out there.

The one thing I was certain about: Saying no to Memphis was the honest answer. Even if I didn't have a good reason why, even if I wasn't happy with the outcome, I knew that saying no came from a place deep inside. I turned and focused on the bridge ahead and let Memphis fade into the distance.

This was the first time in my life since college that I didn't have a plan. On the road, this transition into the unknown felt honest and real. Yet, each time we stopped for the day, my self-doubt bubbled to the surface.

LANDSLIDE

One afternoon, several days into our trip, Mom and I crossed the border into New Mexico. The sun was coming down like a ball of fire. The landscape had been reduced to a silhouette and I could barely keep my eyes open. Peeking through tiny slits in my eyelids, I saw a road sign for a gas station and a Holiday Inn. I braced myself and waited for Mom's voice through the speakers of the walkie-talkie.

"Angie, I can't see. We need to exit and get a hotel." I looked at the clock. It was only 4:30 and we were still two hours away from Albuquerque, my desired destination for the day. I wanted to be sympathetic; after all, I couldn't see either. And when you're in the middle of nowhere, good hotels are hard to find. I knew all of this, but at this point, I didn't want to hear it.

"Are you kidding me?" I yelled into the walkie-talkie and threw it into the floorboard. Startled by my own outburst, I understood that I was upset and frustrated for reasons that did—and didn't—have to do with my mom and her desire to break our massive trip into tiny little bites. I was tired of feeling caught in the middle. Mom trailing behind. Shawn just out of reach. I wanted to go at my own pace.

I pulled into the Holiday Inn parking lot, climbed down from the driver seat, gripped my wallet and refused to look in Mom's direction as I stormed past her car. When I reached the door to the hotel lobby, I grabbed the handle attempting to fling it open in dramatic protest, but it was too heavy. Suddenly I felt ridiculous for throwing a tantrum. Once inside, I got myself together.

"Do you have any rooms with two double beds?" I asked the woman behind the counter. She said yes and I handed over my credit card. Guests hovered by the coffee stand, the television buzzed lightly in the background and the elevator dinged as the doors opened and closed. I noted the stark contrast between the welcoming atmosphere and the battle inside my own mind. I relaxed.

I took the room keys and walked back through the parking lot and prepared to face my mom. I was ready to let it go. But she wouldn't look at me. We rolled our suitcases into the room without a word. Finally, I said, "How long are you going to go without speaking to me?"

She narrowed her eyes, pinning me with her glare. "You've never treated me like this before," she growled. "Who do you think you are?" Her tears started coming and when they started, they didn't stop. She didn't even know me anymore. She called me heartless. Cold. The barrage flooded me; I went numb inside, unable to respond. A protective wall constructed itself around my emotions and I was outside my body, watching the scene unfold.

I'd acted like a brat when she wanted to stop for the day and I didn't feel great about that. My reaction was rude, immature. Why didn't I have more self-control? If I could rewind the clock, I'd have chosen a different response. I would've taken a deep breath and simply said, "OK." I would've made sure we were all clear before I shrieked in frustration and chucked the walkie-talkie. I would've composed myself before getting out of the truck. She would've never known how irritated I was, and I would've gotten over it.

Once, Mom had told me the story about how, when I was 4, I got angry about something—about what I don't know. "You gritted your teeth and screamed so loud the veins popped out of your neck. You looked at me with John eyes," she said. "And I slapped you across the face."

I keyed in on "John eyes." For the most part, she said I seemed so well-adjusted, so happy. But shortly after my mom and John separated, I started crying at random times for no obvious reason and had that temper tantrum. Mom took me to a child psychologist. I remember playing with the toys in the waiting room, but I don't remember what we talked about.

But what about her trauma? Did she ever seek help, support? I'd overheard her crying on the phone to my grandmother and Mom had told me herself: She said John ripped off her bathing suit top and ground her face in the beach sand, wrapped a phone cord around her neck.

It seemed that what she always wanted was a witness. She wanted someone to see her, validate her experience and tell her that she was worthy of love. I'd spent my life trying to show her that she was. I hadn't behaved well. And I may have hurt her in that moment. But I was starting to see that maybe I wasn't the source of this deep pain she continued to carry. Just as I was beginning to recognize that I had my own pain to deal with. Why did this pain continue to resurface? Was it ever OK for me to get angry? If anger is never allowed to be expressed, where does it go?

Inward. Until it erupts.

Finally, I said, "Mom, our relationship is so complicated. It's more than I can take sometimes." This was as close to the truth as I could get, and it was the first time I really admitted to myself that our relationship WAS complicated.

Mom continued to cry. "When we drove by those people on the side of the road ... they were dead. And you acted like it was no big deal. You acted like you didn't even care!"

"What are you talking about?" What was she talking about? At this point we sat on our beds facing each other and I searched my brain, confused. I remembered the traffic jam we'd seen earlier that day. It was on the other side of the highway and my eyes were focused on the road ahead. I didn't know what had caused the backup. I also didn't see any indication that anyone had died. "Mom, I had no idea," I said.

"It was awful. You're out there thinking you're invincible and you're not. That could have been us."

I didn't think I was invincible. But it was true that I wasn't scared, not scared to drive a moving truck and tow a car across the country, anyway. My entire future felt uncertain and that was scary as hell, but the driving made me feel strong.

Finally, I said. "Mom, that accident. That wasn't us. We're OK. We're fine."

As quickly as the fight had escalated, it was over. That's the way it always was with us. Twenty minutes later, we sat at a table in a Tex-Mex restaurant inside the hotel.

"What can I get you ladies to drink?" asked the happy waitress. Mom ordered a margarita. On the rocks with salt.

"Make it two," I said. "But no salt."

The waitress returned with our drinks and we said a toast.

"To us!"

"Here, here!"

Across the room, a band set up to perform. Country music played in the background; it was a song by Travis Tritt about a good-looking woman who was nothing but trouble. I grabbed a spoon from the table—an impromptu microphone. I knew all the words. Mom threw back her head and laughed.

✦

Three days later, we passed the sign that said, "Welcome to Oregon."

I'd read on a travel website, "Oregon is a place where people often find themselves roaming endlessly with no other goal than the next great meal, powdery slope and lighthouse view." The idea of that sounded heavenly, even romantic. A part of me wanted to be that open to possibilities. Already, Shawn had his finger on the pulse of life as an Oregonian. He told me he enjoyed work and the challenge it provided, but people in Portland didn't ask him what he did for a living—they asked him what he did for fun. I was curious about this new life Shawn and Chris were experiencing and the happiness they seemed to have discovered. I wondered if Portland held happiness for me, too.

Suddenly, I realized I was heading downhill, down what felt like a never-ending mountain. I was picking up speed. It took a moment to process this, to realize what was happening. I let off the gas, but I wasn't slowing down. I tapped the brakes and the whole truck shook, wheels grinding in protest. I held my breath. I tried again, released the gas, tapped the brakes—

more grinding and shaking. Now, I started to panic. I noticed a yellow sign signaling an emergency exit ramp to my right, a gravel pit to halt runaway trucks. I thought: Oh shit. I'm the runaway truck. The gravel pit was there for people like me, for such a time as this. My mind raced. I didn't know how to take an emergency exit. What if I crashed into the woods? And how would I reverse and get back on the highway? I didn't know how to reverse this big thing with a car strapped to the back. I didn't know how to slow down.

Instinctively and without really thinking, I shifted to a lower gear. The truck responded, decelerating rapidly. The momentum pushed my body forward; the seatbelt locked in place. I shifted back to drive. Tapped the brakes again. The truck slowed down, agreeable this time. But within seconds it picked up speed. At some point I started breathing again. I tapped the brakes, downshifted, tapped the brakes again and shifted back to drive. I did this again and again for what felt like miles.

The highway leveled out and I was at the bottom. I heard the music coming out of my tiny pink boombox, as if my ears had turned back on. I unwrapped my fingers from the steering wheel and grabbed the walkie-talkie. "Mom, I made it. Are you OK?"

"I'm right behind you. Thank God." She sounded remarkably calm given the circumstances.

I looked around at the small town, with a stoplight and gas station up ahead. Gray-blue skies and mountains painted the horizon. A return to normal, no outward signal of having almost died. I wasn't invincible. Like Thelma and Louise, I could've flown right over the edge. The difference is, they did that by choice. My inclination was to hold on, to stay alive, to make it.

When we arrived in Portland the next morning, two days later than I'd hoped, it was raining. Shawn and Chris had just enough time to unhook my car from the moving truck and get Mom's boxes inside her apartment before they went to work. Everything else would have to wait.

After we all parted ways, I drove the moving truck to Shawn and Chris' apartment, my new home. I found a parking spot on the street and stepped outside. I looked up and could see the rooftop deck at the top of the high-rise and remembered how it had felt during my first trip to Portland to visit Shawn. I wanted to feel like I did that day in the sun, Shawn's arm draped casually over my shoulder. My mind had been as clear as the early September sky.

I stood on the street for another minute, allowing the soft drizzle to hit my cheeks and run down my face. The rain felt like tears, but I couldn't bring myself to cry.

IDLE

November in Portland had a different vibe. A soft, constant drizzle replaced the summer sun. Our window-abundant apartment, now washed in gray, matched my new mood. Nothing came of my interview at Shawn's station and none of the other stations my agent contacted had responded. While Shawn, Chris and Mom went to work each day, I slept until 11 a.m. It wasn't a restful sleep. I couldn't bring myself to get out of bed. As winter approached and the sun set earlier each day, I averaged about five hours of daylight. I spent those hours wandering around the apartment, wondering what to do with myself. My first impulse was to shop, but I had no money.

Shawn's solution to our new one-income life was to sell his Jeep. He told me over the phone, during his lunch break. My heart sank. I thought of the summer we bought it. He'd remove the top and both doors, toss the surfboard in the back and drive to Folly Beach to catch a few waves before work.

"You can't sell the Jeep," I said. "You love that thing."

"I don't need it," he replied, unaffected. I imagined him sitting in his director's chair in the control room surrounded by buttons and monitors, his face void of expression, or any emotion whatsoever. "I walk everywhere. And you have a car. We don't need two."

"If I had a job, you wouldn't have to sell it." I felt guilty. Shawn's decision to sell the Jeep was my fault. Since I was 16, I'd never not worked and I could feel the shame about my idleness blooming inside me.

"True, but we still don't need two cars. The Jeep served its purpose. It was fun while we were in Charleston. Here, it's just sitting on the street."

Before leaving Charleston, I'd sold furniture because it wouldn't fit into the moving truck. Now, Chris' futon was the centerpiece of our living room and my clothes hung in the coat closet in the hall. The king-sized bed Shawn and I bought for our new house took up so much space in the tiny Portland bedroom there was no room to walk. Everything else was in storage. It seemed as if we were slowly deconstructing everything that we'd worked so hard to build. But Shawn didn't seem to mind at all. I didn't understand this about him. How could he let go? How could he say goodbye so easily?

One afternoon, I stood at the window and watched Shawn standing on the sidewalk 10 floors down. He shook hands with a woman and handed her the keys to his Jeep. She drove away and I said goodbye to another piece of our old life in Charleston.

✦

I needed to put my energy somewhere. When I was in high school, I loved waking up at sunrise on summer mornings and driving to cheerleading practice, preparing for camp. At camp the summer before my senior year, a few of my varsity teammates and I got picked to join the Universal Cheerleading Association's All-Star Team and flew to London to perform in the New Year's Day parade. Cheerleading opened up a whole new world for me.

Working on camera was a different type of performance. Regardless of whether I engaged in light banter with my co-anchors on the morning show or reported about an approaching hurricane while bracing myself against high winds and gripping my baseball cap—I worked to maintain an element of control, presenting the most polished, professional version of myself. When I cheered and danced, I got to move, smile and emote as much as I wanted, as big as the beat of the hip-hop music and the marching band.

I couldn't think of any way to replicate it, to fill that void. I accepted that my dancing days were over. That is, until I spontaneously searched online and found a listing for Viscount Dance Studios on East Burnside. They offered adult hip-hop classes once a week.

One Monday night, I walked into a class, took my place in front of the mirror, and attempted to mimic the moves of our instructor, a cute sprout of a woman named Edie. Edie might've been my age, but she expressed the confidence and energy level of a teenager. Her dark brown hair was pulled into a ponytail on the top of her head and she wore a sky-blue sun visor. I was immediately drawn to her, the way she breezed into the studio. The pep in her step.

As I attempted to twist, turn, pop and shake my booty like I was in high school again, I realized a few things. Number one: Somewhere, deep down in there, I still had it. Two: I was painfully out of practice. And three: I felt surprisingly self-conscious.

Back in my cheerleading days, we'd practice one eight-count over and over until our motions were sharp and in sync. In Edie's dance class, she'd show us a step once and move on to the next. I couldn't pick up on the routine that quickly. I felt like I was doing the African Anteater Ritual from the movie "Can't Buy Me Love" while Edie and the dancers around me could've easily performed backup in the latest Britney Spears video.

For the entire hour, I danced, felt weird, and tried to figure out who this person in the mirror was. I'd imagined how taking this $10-a-week dance class would make me feel, as if it had some magical power to zap me into a new and improved, sexy, fun and carefree version of myself. Moving my body to music was, in fact, shaking off the cobwebs of depression, at least for the moment. But my reflection kept throwing me off. I didn't enjoy watching myself. When I performed during football games in high school, I made eye contact with the cheering crowd. I missed performing. More specifically, I missed the connection. I missed my team. I missed my co-workers. I missed my friends and our life back in Charleston. Here, in this class full of strangers and in the shadow of Edie's sparkling presence, away from the camaraderie and the applause, I felt alone.

✦

I also worried that word would get back to people in Charleston that I was, essentially, doing nothing productive with my time. I explained this to Stephanie when she called one day. I was excited to talk to her because Don had just proposed.

Before Stephanie and Don moved to Charleston, Stephanie worked as a television news reporter at a station five hours south of Portland, in Medford, Oregon. Don worked in San Francisco, and they maintained a long-distance relationship for a couple of years. Then, Don got the news director job in Charleston, and they decided Stephanie would quit her job in Medford and come with him. When we met, she was unemployed and dodging the uncomfortable cocktail party question, "So. What do you do?"

"Tell them you're a socialite," Don said. "That will shut them up."

Stephanie was a smart, college-educated woman with her own career, and she said she didn't enjoy being perceived as Don's tag-along. Eventually, after months of torturous waiting, Stephanie got hired as a reporter for the local ABC station. Now, Stephanie said, those days spent worrying about her future seemed so far away. She'd bounced back in her career, quickly. She was about to get married.

"Angie, spend all day in your pajamas," she advised. "Who cares? You'll be back at work soon enough and then you'll kick yourself for not enjoying this time."

"You're so right," I said looking down at my attire and the state of my sad, unshowered self—plaid drawstring pants, tank top, no bra. My cute, sassy haircut had lost its shape and my roots were showing. I wanted to be OK with this version of me, to learn how to relax into the not knowing, but the thing I wasn't telling anyone is that the depression was getting more and more difficult to shake off. After years of living in the spotlight, I was floundering in the dark.

"So, the reason I called," Stephanie said, changing the subject. "Would you like to be in my wedding? Will you be a bridesmaid?" She told me the wedding date was set for the following October in her hometown in New York state.

"Oh my goodness! Yes!" The invitation gave me a lift. Turns out, I did have a life. It just happened to be 3,000 miles away.

After Stephanie and I hung up, I turned on the television to watch the noon newscast on Shawn's station. The anchors looked so warm and cozy sitting behind the desk inside the climate-controlled studio. The reporters, however, wore The North Face jackets and stood outside in the rain. I grabbed a blanket and the remote, plopped down on the futon and switched the channel to E!

DARKNESS

"We need to get away," Shawn proposed one day. "I've been looking online and I think we should spend a couple of days in McMinnville. There's a place called Hotel Oregon. It looks pretty cool."

"I'll check my calendar, but I'm sure I'm free," I joked.

In fact, the romantic gesture woke me up inside. Finally, something to look forward to. But days later, when Shawn and I arrived in the quiet town, another wave of depression washed over me. It was drizzling, and something about the atmosphere, the quiet, made me sad. I didn't want Shawn to think I was disappointed in this trip he'd planned, so I stuffed down the lump in my throat and quashed the fire burning in my chest.

We carried our bags into the room and Shawn beamed, so proud he'd discovered this place. The hotel was almost a hundred years old, with European-style decor and hardwood floors. The room had a king-sized bed and its own private bath, which was an upgrade.

"This is awesome," he said.

"Yeah, it is," I said and immediately felt ashamed of myself, pretending to be fine when I wasn't. Shawn had put so much thought into this getaway. I kept looking for something—anything—that felt familiar. I felt swallowed up by too much change at once.

We dropped our bags and headed upstairs to the rooftop bar to have lunch. Our table for two on the outdoor deck revealed a view of the wine country. The rain had subsided and sun rays broke through the clouds. Shawn looked relaxed. Moving to Portland had done something to him; it was as if his whole perspective on life had changed. I was just noticing all this now, the difference in Shawn. I finally saw how unhappy he'd grown during those last months in Charleston. It's not like we never talked about it, but perhaps I'd been so focused on trying to get him to see me, to understand, I'd not done enough to see and understand him. I thought we knew each other so well, but we'd traveled to new territory— geographically, and in our relationship.

"What do you think?" he asked, admiring the scenery, a bright and airy contrast to the dark hotel.

"This is great. It really is." This response felt true. I loved being on a rooftop with a view. I thought for a moment, wondering how I might try to let Shawn in. "I just feel so out of place," I said. "I feel like I've been stripped of my identity. I don't know who I am."

As quickly as I said it, an internal voice said: That's not true; you're right here. It was difficult to describe, this voice

I was noticing. It felt like a thought. But I could also hear it, somewhere in my soul.

Shawn was quiet, pondering my confession about feeling lost. "I get it. Just give it time. This is a terrible time of year to get a job. No one's hiring. Something will happen after the holidays." He wasn't stressed about it. He didn't mind the fact that I wasn't working. We'd adjusted our expenses. We'd gotten rid of a car payment. We were splitting rent with Chris.

Shawn didn't want anything from me, except to be in that moment with him. I decided to try. After lunch at Hotel Oregon, Shawn suggested we check out the wine country. We hopped back in the car and drove for a while. We ended up at Amity Vineyards. The grapes had been harvested and the vines along the winding roads were mostly bare. We headed straight to the tasting room.

The woman inside welcomed us and immediately began lining bottles along the counter and explaining what they were: riesling, pinot blanc, gewürztraminer, chardonnay and the vineyard's famous pinot noir. With each pour, as our resident wine expert discussed tannins and oak, Shawn swirled the wine, stuck his nose in the glass and rolled the beverage around in his mouth. He was fully present, all five senses engaged.

I participated in the occasion by being in two places at once. Inside and outside of my body. In the moment but somewhere else. In the moment, I discovered I preferred pinot noir because I thought it was smooth and smelled like flowers. I wondered if I said that in a restaurant—can I have a glass of wine that's smooth and smells like flowers?—would the waiter know what I was talking about? But I also felt like I was watching some other couple I didn't recognize taste wine. Who were these people touring the wine country? What were we even doing right now? In the back of my mind, I had this gnawing feeling like I was running out of time. Like I didn't have a right to be there, enjoying myself, when there was still so much to figure out. I didn't realize that the very thing I resisted—letting things be unresolved and relaxing into the moment—was the thing I needed most. I needed to awaken my senses and experience simple pleasures without shame or guilt for not doing something more productive with my life. I needed to take some tips from that travel website and "roam endlessly with no other goal." But I couldn't relax. If I relaxed, I feared, my life would spin out of control.

Back at the hotel, we ventured downstairs to The Cellar Bar, which was decorated like a 1920s speakeasy. I looked around at the tables all around the room. "There's nobody here." The words played in my head, on repeat. Literally no one else. The bartender slid us two beers on tap. Shawn swiveled his bar stool toward me and leaned back into the seat.

"You look so happy," I said, holding onto so much sadness, trying not to burst. "You seem like you're having a really good time."

"I am."

My goal-driven, always-moving-forward husband had hit his stride. He'd always said he didn't want to get comfortable, in work or in life. This move to Portland had satisfied something that had been missing for him.

When I'd stood on the apartment rooftop months earlier, I told myself I wanted to slow down. I wanted to feel free. So, I quit my job and moved to Portland, fantasizing about how every day could feel like a Friday, how Shawn and I could run away for the weekend anytime we wanted. And now, Portland was the last place I wanted to be. I thought it would make me happy—as happy as Shawn appeared to be now. Why did we have to move so far away from home for him to finally be happy? He was living in the moment and I was dying in it, falling into an abyss of despair. I couldn't have predicted this, how this move would unleash such a black hole of darkness in me, engulfing me in sorrow I'd masked for years. What was the point in chasing a dream when in the end, when the lights go out and the curtain is pulled back, you realized that your success—everything you thought you had become—was nothing more than smoke and mirrors?

A half hour later, we walked up to the hotel restaurant on the first floor and slid into a booth overlooking the street.

The road, too, was empty. I stared out the window, desperately trying to hold it together.

"Talk to me," Shawn said.

But how? How could I talk to him about this? What would I even say? "Shawn, I'm so sorry. I love you for planning this trip." I cracked. Tears escaped from my eyes.

He reached across the table and placed his hand on top of mine. He was hurt. I had hurt him. I pressed my fingers into my eyes, trying to stop the flood. I was ruining our date and couldn't do a thing about it.

"Do we need to go?" he asked. I nodded my head yes. The waitress walked up to the table and I turned my face toward the window, attempting to hide. Shawn asked for the check and a couple of to-go boxes. "We're going to take this back to the room," he said.

After dinner, I crawled into bed and hid my face in the pillow. Shawn sat beside me and rubbed my back until I eventually fell asleep.

The next morning, we drove home in silence. There wasn't anything to say. The trip was a disaster, and it was my fault. When Shawn and I got back to the apartment, Chris was sitting in the recliner watching TV.

"Hey, what's up? How was it?" he asked.

I forced a smile, covering my swollen eyes behind a pair of sunglasses, which were totally unnecessary in Oregon in November, and inside the apartment in particular. "It was good," I said, answering before Shawn had a chance. Then, I quickly changed the subject, "What have you been up to?"

Once Shawn and Chris started talking, I excused myself and darted to the bedroom. I pretended that Chris didn't notice, as if masks can keep people from seeing right through you.

UNTANGLING

Wherever we worked, Shawn and I had always been known as the station's TV couple. To my male co-workers, I was just one of the guys, or perhaps a work sister. A few of them, including my morning show co-anchor who lived in the "Melrose Place" apartment complex, became my close friends. It was quite common to make eye contact across the cubicles in the late afternoon after being at work since 4 a.m., and for one of us say to the other, "I need a beer," which would result in a happy hour on someone's screened porch overlooking the parking lot.

So it shouldn't have felt awkward to have Chris as a roommate. He was just as respectful as I'd imagined he'd be. We were careful not to get in each other's way, eat each other's groceries, or leave a mess for the other to deal with. But it did feel awkward. It felt awkward because I no longer felt like the fun work friend. Why would he want to live with a roommate—someone's depressed wife—who was spiraling into a deep, dark funk? I didn't want to do anything or go anywhere. I didn't want Chris to witness my unraveling, which is perhaps why, when I arrived at Hotel Oregon, I promptly fell apart.

I sensed that Chris knew what was going on, although he never acted any different. One day, Chris invited me to take a road trip over the Washington state border to see Mount St. Helens. I wanted to say no, but I mustered enough energy to get dressed and go. I was secretly glad when we arrived at the observation park and discovered it was closed for the day. I wouldn't have to get out of the car; I was relieved to keep riding and staring out the window.

Chris didn't seem to mind hanging out with this boring version of me, or perhaps he didn't have a lot of options either. On the car ride back, I felt compelled to open up. "I just don't feel like myself anymore," I confessed. "I feel lost. Like I don't know where I'm going."

"Why don't you try to stop thinking about everything so much?" Chris asked, in a way that made me curious and not defensive.

I noticed how my mind was clinging to its thoughts, refusing to release its grip. I didn't understand why the wise voice I'd recently noticed only popped in every now and then. Where was she now? Why did she always disappear when I needed her?

I noticed how, when something felt true, my mind and body felt expansive. Most other times, my insides felt like a pressure cooker. Back in Charleston after I got the job offer in Memphis, the minister's sermon had challenged me to let go of the nets. I didn't fully understand what that meant, but

I did the next thing that felt right: I turned down the job. I moved to Portland. And what good did that do? There I was, 3,000 miles away from home, still trapped in those nets.

I needed to let go. I needed to let go of my unruly thoughts and the idea of how I thought my love story with Shawn—and our success story—would unfold. I just didn't know how. Or, perhaps, I didn't trust where letting go would lead. If I stopped trying to control my future, where would I end up? The thought made me shudder.

For the rest of the car ride, I tried to practice not overthinking. I focused on the song on the radio. I turned my attention to Chris. He liked his job. He missed his friends. He felt lonely too.

✦

On Thanksgiving Day, Shawn, Chris and I stood around the kitchen counter of Mom's Portland townhouse and took turns saying what we were thankful for. It was unanimous. We were grateful for Mom's juicy turkey and famous macaroni and cheese. And we acknowledged the mutual appreciation for each other—our West Coast modern family.

After dinner, the guys left for work. Mom and I hauled boxes of Christmas decorations from the garage and up the stairs to the living room. Back in Charleston, Mom's trees towered to the ceilings. She'd spend an entire weekend arguing with Patrick over the lights (the plug always ended up at the top of the tree instead of the bottom) and meticulously placing the ornaments. She'd hook one ornament to a branch and step back—to ensure symmetry—before adding another. But this year, in her tiny townhouse, Mom concluded a smaller tree was in order. We'd gone to a tree farm and picked it out, and there it stood—bare and barely 5 feet tall—in the corner of the room.

I dug through one of the boxes and found a cassette tape—Kenny Rogers and Dolly Parton's soundtrack from the movie "A Christmas to Remember." The tape had belonged to my grandmother. I turned on the stereo, popped in the cassette and pressed play. As Kenny and Dolly sang about having springtime feelings in December, my thoughts shifted to Patrick.

I recalled the first Christmas after my grandmother died. I was home from college and buried under the covers of my warm, comfortable bed.

"Ho! Ho! Ho!" It was still dark outside, but Patrick's booming voice shook me out of a deep sleep. I lifted my head. Patrick stood over me donning a Santa hat and holding a video camera. The red light glowed. Like Rudolph. "Ho! Ho! Ho!" he announced again. "Merry Christmas!"

"Merry Christmas," I croaked, shaking off the sleep. I hid my face in the pillow before finally giving into his jolly making. "OK, I'm getting up." When I made it out to the living room, the smell of freshly brewed coffee filled the air. Kenny and Dolly serenaded us.

Patrick's gift choices were always questionable. That particular year, he'd bought my mom a wet/dry razor. I gazed into the video camera and held the box up like Vanna White. In my best announcer voice I explained, "Now, you can shave your legs in the shower, in the kitchen, and even when you're driving down the road!" Still living in the shadow of mourning and missing my grandmother so much, it felt good to laugh.

As Mom and I prepared for our first Christmas in Portland, I smiled at the memory, but it wasn't enough to shake off the dull ache. Mom felt it too.

We pulled ornaments out of the boxes and unwrapped them one by one. And there it was. The Santa hat that Patrick always wore. Mom lifted it up and held it for a moment. She didn't say a word, but I knew. She missed him.

✦

On Christmas morning, Mom drove to our apartment. I played music, started the coffee and cooked a big southern breakfast: bacon, eggs, grits and toast. I hoped to keep the mood upbeat, as if I were in charge of Christmas spirit. I acted the way I wanted to feel and so far, it was working. Mom, on the other hand, was quiet, barely holding it together.

We'd planned to spend the day at Mount Hood, and later that morning I rode with Mom back to her townhouse so she could drop off her car and change clothes. In her living room, she set down her purse and paused by the 5-foot tree. She didn't need my holiday cheer. She needed me to be real. "Mom, what's going on?" I asked.

She sucked in her breath. I wrapped my arms around her and she buried her head in my shoulder and let out a muffled sob. I hadn't told her about my meltdown at Hotel Oregon, so she didn't know how much I understood. Finally, she looked at me and said, "I want to go home."

I felt a rush of relief. This relief, I sensed, was a deep knowing that staying in Portland wouldn't be good for her. Going home was exactly what Mom needed to do. "Mom, if you want to go home, go home! You can quit your job, pack your bags, and get out of here. You don't have to stay."

When my grandmother died, the grief came swift like a sucker punch. Losing her had shaken my foundation. I believed that when I moved away to college, it compounded her sadness and made her sick. When I decided to transfer to the University of South Carolina, I told her, "I'll be so much closer now!" As if that would've made it better. As if it wasn't already too late.

That was the real reason I never questioned Mom's idea to move to Portland. If she moved to Portland with me, I could keep her close. If I kept her close, nothing would happen to her. But Mom wasn't my grandmother. Mom wanted to live. I was no longer a child, clinging to her legs, trying to protect her, trying to make the bad things stop. It was time to release my grip and give her space to fight for her own life.

"I can't leave you here," she said. She was still trying to save me, too.

"Yes, you can. I'm going to be fine."

"I feel like a failure. I'm quitting on our plan."

"Mom, it's OK to turn around and go back. We have choices," I said, the deep knowing rising up. Mom had always pushed me so hard to make sure I had choices. She didn't realize that she had choices too. I said it again. "We always have choices."

Mom had poured her unrealized goals and dreams into me. I'd held on to her, not knowing who I was, or what to do or be in the world without her by my side. Now it was time to untangle ourselves. She needed to go home. I needed to stay. We had to face this part of the journey on our own.

SPLINTS

The next week, Mom turned in her notice at work. For the return trip to Charleston, she opted out of the scenic drive. She hired movers, decided to ship her car, and booked her plane ticket home.

A few days before Mom left Portland, we had lunch at the Pilsner Room, a restaurant and bar on the waterfront. Shawn stopped by her townhouse to get a large palm plant that I'd agreed to adopt because it wouldn't survive the move. When Shawn stopped by the restaurant to return Mom's key, I met him outside, so he didn't have to search for a parking space. That's when I noticed the plant, stuffed sideways in the backseat. Some of the limbs had snapped.

"You broke her plant!" I stood there for a moment, stunned. "You broke the plant! You broke my mom's plant." I couldn't stop saying the same thing, over and over. "Shawn, how could you?"

"What?" he said.

I opened the back passenger side door of my Hyundai and pointed to the mangled tree. "Look! You just stuffed it in there. The branches are broken."

"Sorry," he muttered, finally.

"Just go," I whispered, walking back inside the restaurant and leaving him standing there.

"What happened?" Mom asked when I returned to the table.

"He broke your plant!"

"Angie, it's just a plant," she said.

"No, it's not just a plant. It's YOUR plant."

I was so mad it was starting to feel funny. Like I might laugh and cry. It was, in fact, just a plant. I'd never owned a plant. I wasn't even sure how to take care of it. But for as long as I was able to keep it alive, it would brighten up the apartment. And Shawn had stuffed it in the car, like it didn't matter that much. Like it didn't matter at all.

"Oh, sweetie," she said, looking sympathetic. "Angie, you're so much like me. You're being too hard on him. He loves you."

I sat silent. I didn't have the energy to argue my point. Maybe I was just like her. I knew I'd overreacted. I knew Shawn loved me. But still, I couldn't let it go. Why couldn't he understand why a simple houseplant mattered so much?

When I got back to the apartment after lunch, I found Shawn sitting on the futon, staring at the television. He didn't seem to be watching anything. I noticed the plant perched under a window, branches intact. Confused, I walked over to investigate. Shawn had repaired the broken limbs with Scotch tape and toothpicks. Tiny splints. I placed my hand over my mouth and tried to mask the smile.

He did understand. The plant mattered because it mattered to me. It was worth the effort. I walked over to the futon and kissed the top of Shawn's head. "Thank you for fixing the plant."

"You're welcome," he said, all defenses dropped. "I'm sorry."

"Yeah, me too. Me too." I sat down beside him, joining him in the silence as he flipped channels. The broken plant, and Shawn's attempt to mend it, said more to me than words ever could.

It was time to face this part of the journey—just the two of us—together.

REGRETS

About a month after Mom moved back to Charleston, I flew home for a visit. She'd rented a two-bedroom apartment in a golf course community close to the townhouse where we lived when I was in high school after she and Cam split up. It felt good to be back home and spending time in the neighborhoods where I grew up, where memories of high school echoed as I drove down the streets. Memories of fun times with friends felt so close.

Mom set up the guest bedroom with a daybed and old family photos. The attached bathroom was decorated in purples and pinks, seashells and beach art. Nesting came so naturally to her. Perhaps she never realized that all I ever wanted was to feel at home inside my own life.

The next day, I made plans to have breakfast with my friend Jeané, the morning show producer at Channel 5. She knew me like other people didn't. She saw me in the middle of the night with no makeup and curlers in my hair. She ignored me when I complained about typos and inconsistencies in the scripts. And she listened when I was in knots over my wedding and my decision not to invite my birth father, John.

As a teenager, I'd been left to negotiate my relationship with John on my own. He started reaching out again when I was in high school, after my grandfather died and Mom and Cam got divorced. I told him that I accepted his apologies while attempting to hold some boundaries (before I'd ever heard of the word, much less understood what it meant).

John got sober and started going to church. Years later, he'd begin to come to terms with the fact that he'd been abused too. For decades, he believed that the abuse was his fault, that he'd allowed it to happen. I understood all of this—pain and suffering doesn't happen in a vacuum. It's passed down from generation to generation. I didn't object to him being back in my life on a limited basis, but sometimes, the relationship pushed up against the edges of my comfort zone. I was still trying to come to terms with things, too. And there was Mom, who got mad every time John called. She would remind me of all the things he'd done to us, as if I'd forgotten.

When I was 16, John offered to buy me a car, a used Toyota Camry. It was old but reliable and something neither Mom nor Cam could afford. Mom agreed that it would be helpful if I had a car; I'd been borrowing hers to drive to work and cheerleading. Mom told me to call Cam to get his temperature on John's offer.

Cam said, "I wish I could buy you a car, but I can't. Let him do it."

Later, after I graduated from college, John offered to pay off my student loans. I'd budgeted for the loan payments, but with my entry-level salary it would take 10 years to repay the debt. John said he owed it to me. It was the child support he never paid. Mom and Cam agreed.

I'd hoped these gifts didn't come with strings attached, but also, I let John know how much I appreciated it. I continued to keep our relationship separate from the other parts of my life, but things came to a head just before Shawn and I got married. John wanted to go to the wedding; he said he'd sit in the back of the church and skip the reception if that's what I wanted. That seemed OK with me. Mom wasn't having it. She couldn't be in the same room with him. Many people in our family didn't know, or didn't believe, that she was abused and never understood, or just didn't try to understand, why John lost custody of me. The thought of him at the wedding shaking hands with people made Mom boil. She was so upset about it that she called Cam, which led to Cam calling me at work one morning. He never called me at work.

"Hey, Ang, this is your dad," he said, which is what he always said. But his voice was different, fragile. He told me he'd talked to my mom. "I'm not saying you can't invite him." He didn't say John's name and he stopped short of saying, "But it's him or me." "I just feel like ..." He paused for several seconds, and I thought we'd gotten disconnected.

"You're my daughter ..." His voice cracked as the emotions he rarely expressed and the words I'd longed to hear caught in his throat.

I was undone.

I decided that I was with Mom and Cam on this. They were still in so much pain. I couldn't do this to them. My wedding day was not the time for a reunion. I couldn't let these deep wounds from the past creep into my new beginning with Shawn. I didn't know yet that they'd creep in, anyway.

In the weeks that followed, I got tangled up in a series of emotional conversations with John. I got letters from his family, people who I loved, telling me how much he'd changed. I knew they meant well, but I didn't cause the situation. Why was it on me to fix it? In one of our final emails, I asked John, "Have you ever thought about how I feel?"

He replied, "I think you're still angry."

That did make me angry. He didn't get it. No one did. No one, I believed, understood how I really felt. Unseen. They saw what was on the outside. My performance. The role I played. No one ever seemed to understand what was going on inside of me.

It was a complex triangle of emotions: my loyalty to mom, my yearning for Cam, and my unresolved feelings for John. I was trying to find some sort of middle ground between letting him back in my life like nothing ever happened and shutting him out completely.

Jeané became my sounding board. After the morning show, I'd walk up to the producer desk and sit at the computer station next to her. "I don't know what to do," I said.

She agreed that I was still angry. "Angie, you need to forgive him," she said.

I thought I had forgiven John. I'd tried to be a good person, but I didn't know how to separate my feelings from everyone else's. I didn't want to cause any more pain, and that was at the heart of my conflict. I couldn't see that I was being put in an impossible situation.

"Forgiveness isn't for the other person," Jeané said. "It doesn't absolve them of what they did wrong. Finding forgiveness is for you."

After the wedding, John moved to Costa Rica. Before he left, I invited him to lunch at a restaurant on Shem Creek. He was visibly guarded. After lunch, in the parking lot, I told him that I was sorry about what happened before the wedding. I still wasn't sure if it was my fault, or anyone's fault. I was just sorry that it happened, sorry about so much emotional carnage. "I forgive you for what happened when I was a child. And I need you to release yourself from the need to keep apologizing to me about it."

I didn't know which specific details he remembered about the abuse and rage. I didn't know which memories he blocked out, or which ones he couldn't admit. Still, I believed him when he said he held himself responsible. I'd seen in his face, many times, the expression of what I interpreted to be true remorse. He said if he could go back and undo all of it, he would. But that just wasn't possible.

I continued, "Things are the way they are because of what happened in the past. But I'm not holding a grudge. You deserve to find your own peace." His eyes welled up with tears. "You need to free yourself, too. The only thing we can do is move forward from here."

I knew I'd searched my heart and found the words that finally felt like mine, the words that felt true. When I hugged John goodbye, I realized that I'd become my own advocate, the one I needed growing up.

✦

During my short visit home from Portland, I walked into the restaurant and saw Jeané across the room. She waved. I waved back and joined her.

She stood up and gave me a hug. "Hey, girl, what's up? How's life across the country?"

I tried to explain it: Mom moved back, I couldn't find a job, Shawn was happy, most of the time I was not, but I still felt like something important was happening. Sometimes, my life felt like it was falling apart, but maybe it was supposed to. My words got all tangled up, a run-on sentence. My mind was in a swirl.

When I came up for air she asked, "Do you have any regrets?" Jeané had a gift for getting right to the point, the heart of the matter.

I thought for a moment and said, "Yes, I do. I have lots of regrets. I wish things had never changed, but deep down, I know they had to."

I'd loved those days at Channel 5; they were hard and rewarding. My co-workers had given me a work home and a sense of belonging. I would always miss that time in my life. But my heart wanted so much more than makeup and bright lights. It wanted more than a brand-new house. My heart wanted—what? Something that couldn't be mapped out with an action plan. Something that felt elusive, like peace.

✦

My biggest regret, according to my hairdresser, Randall, was the atrocity sprouting from my head. Randall started doing my hair when I anchored the morning show. But now that I was unemployed and living in a city where I only knew approximately four people, I couldn't justify the expensive salon service. Randall had never charged me, which always felt way too generous. He insisted. "You're my tax write-off."

And he knew I'd spread the word when people asked where I got my hair done. But now, I was just making him look bad.

"Girl, I don't know what you've done," he said, "but promise me you won't do it again."

"But Randall, if you had seen that infomercial ..."

"No. Just, no," he said, cutting me off and running his hands through my brassy strands like he was searching for lice. He didn't want to hear about the box color I bought from Walgreens.

Regardless of what Randall thought, there was something liberating about do-it-yourself hair. While watching "American Idol," I'd colored my hair dark like Kelly Clarkson and painted two blond streaks around my face. It was an inexpensive way to change my look, for better or worse, and it was kind of fun. So much fun that during my time playing beauty shop, I considered becoming a hairdresser. I told Randall this.

"Girl, you should do nails. You could rent that space right over there," he said, pointing with his comb at a table across the room. "I could send my clients to you."

I thought about how my grandmother got her license to do nails after my grandfather died. I admired how she dared to try something new, to reinvent herself. "Can you make me look like this?" I asked, changing the subject, not wanting to entertain the fantasy anymore. I held up a page ripped from a magazine featuring Reese Witherspoon, modeling the cute, flippy style she wore in "Sweet Home Alabama."

"I'll try," Randall said. "But we have a lot of work to do."

✦

When my plane landed back in Portland, I noticed a sense of familiarity, like I was visiting a close friend. I grabbed my carry-on and walked in step with the crowd, rolling my luggage through the airport terminal, keeping my eyes open for Shawn. I spotted him beyond the security check, holding a bouquet of yellow roses and a gift bag with a rainbow of tissue paper peeking out from the top. We had yellow roses at our wedding—I chose them because they were my grandmother's favorite, to honor her memory. Now they'd become a symbol of something else. Commitment. Staying together. Even when it's hard.

I was beginning to learn what most married couples must learn—that it takes more than love to sustain the relationship. It takes more than friendship. It takes more than mutual respect. We had all those things. But it never occurred to me that I'd change so drastically. I'm certain it never occurred to him either. We embraced and kissed each other hello, and I took a moment to admire the flowers.

"Go ahead and look," he said, knowing I was dying to peek inside the bag. I pulled out a hardcover book: "What Should I Do With My Life?" by Po Bronson. "I saw him on 'Oprah,'" Shawn said. "It seemed like something you would like."

Shawn didn't watch "Oprah" the way fans watched "Oprah." He simply worked in a newsroom where televisions lined the walls. The Po Bronson segment caught his attention. I looked at him for a moment, deeply moved by his thoughtfulness.

On the car ride back to our apartment, I traced my fingers along the hardcover, read the inside and back flap copy and flipped through the pages. I scanned the chapter titles with interest. The introduction noted that many of us have a need to know where we're headed in the story of our lives—not to spoil the ending, but to know that when the ending comes, it won't be shallow. The author understood the urge for our lives to mean something.

He'd interviewed hundreds of people—people who'd found themselves at a crossroads—and asked them about what had happened next. He discovered that many of us have psychological stumbling blocks—misconceptions and fears—that keep us from walking a path that feels true. When people asked him if the book was about life or about work, he said, "It's about people who dared to be honest with themselves."

These strangers were my people. I needed to know their stories. It wasn't lost on me how much Shawn understood that.

STAY

In February, the six-month lease on our 10th-floor Portland apartment was up. Shawn and I moved to a smaller apartment in the same building, and Chris moved to a one-bedroom unit a few blocks away. This had always been the plan. Shawn and Chris hadn't left me out; they knew I'd get to Portland eventually and our time together as roommates would be temporary. As we packed boxes once again, I realized I'd been short-sighted, so caught up in my own emotions about Shawn leaving Charleston that I couldn't see the big picture. Now, it felt bittersweet saying goodbye to Chris as a roommate, the bigger apartment, and the view of the Portland skyline. I wished I would've relaxed and been mentally present enough to enjoy our time together more, but that was the hindsight talking.

Shawn and I moved down to the third floor. I recognized the floor plan immediately because it was our old apartment cut in half. We'd looked at other open units, and this apartment wasn't my first choice. But Shawn had a vision for our tiny place. He felt the ambiance. The kitchen had a bar overlooking the living room. And the living space was anchored by two big corner windows. Our 10th-floor view had been replaced by shady trees; Shawn said it felt like living in a tree house. He said he could see us sitting at the bar, enjoying dinner and a glass of wine.

We put more of our belongings in storage. As I unpacked a few small boxes of glasses, plates, utensils and only the necessary pots and pans, I realized I was beginning to appreciate the limited space. We were living on less—less stuff and less money. There was something freeing about paring down the excess, reducing our possessions and our expenses to exactly what we needed.

✦

One day, when Shawn was at work, I threw on some sweats and drove to the library on 23rd to check my email. All the computers were occupied, so I added my name to the waiting list and browsed the aisles. Some titles caught my eye. "Get Over It and On With It" and "The Mystery of God's Will." I pulled them off the shelves.

I still had days when I was too depressed to talk on the phone and would let the answering machine pick up. But I looked forward to getting email—to having conversations with my friends and family behind the veil of a computer screen. I didn't feel the pressure to pretend everything was fine, put on a cheery face and add some pep to my voice. Over email, I could sit in silence and think about what I wanted to share and what I wanted to keep private. Still, I craved the interaction, and when a spot at the table came open, my heart rate accelerated as I logged into my email account. Three new messages. Mom. Stephanie. Lindsay.

Lindsay and I worked together at the television station in Columbia and we'd been swapping emails recently. I was eager to read her reply. She'd moved to Nashville and gotten married. She told me she left the local news business and was now a freelance writer and producer, doing celebrity interviews and working for shows on CMT. I was intrigued by this. I envisioned her sitting at home, writing a script on her personal laptop. It reminded me of my early days as a producer, and something about that appealed to me. Lindsay was using her expertise, but in a different way. She told me she didn't miss being in news. I admired her confidence.

I logged off the library computer before my hour was up. After checking out the books I found earlier, I walked a couple of blocks to Starbucks. I ordered a latte and settled into a plush, oversized chair by the window. I opened "Get Over It and On With It" and started reading. The author explained the series of emotions you go through when life as you know it changes suddenly. According to her, the up and down emotions I'd been experiencing were normal. I hadn't considered that. It certainly didn't feel normal.

I lifted my head out of the book and looked around, validated. I was wearing sweatpants and no makeup, my hair twisted up in a clip. I tucked my legs underneath me, sinking deeper into the chair. The sidewalk was busy with pedestrians, and jazz music pumped out of the coffee shop speakers. I wondered if it would be possible to accept where I was now, to really believe that my personal and professional unraveling was for the best.

I wrote that in my journal. Then I paused, something inside me shifting. I was suddenly comfortable, in that chair and in my own skin. I recognized this feeling. This was exactly how I felt those nights at the university library, typing essays for my creative nonfiction writing class. Now, holding my pen—journal in my lap and a hot latte by my side—for the first time in a long time, I was content. I wrote that down too. I wanted to document the moment, so I'd recognize the feeling when it returned.

✦

When I got home that afternoon, I stopped to check the mail. I flipped through the stack and stopped at a letter for me. From Los Angeles. From the talent agency that represented me. I ripped open the envelope.

It was a one-paragraph letter in carefully crafted legal speak. The message was straightforward. The words "no longer" and "your agent" jumped off the page. Andrew had left the agency, and the agency had dropped me from their client list.

I felt myself deflate. At this level of my career, it was important to have an agent. On-air talent, as we were often called, rarely moved up to bigger television markets without agent representation. It wasn't impossible, but having an agent certainly helped. Agents had the connections; agents negotiated the deals.

The prestigious Los Angeles talent agency that had also represented my professional idol, Nancy O'Dell, had let me go. If I'd not just had that quiet revelation in Starbucks, I might've been more upset. Now I could see that they'd done me a favor. After the initial wave of disappointment, I felt lighter. Perhaps my life and career weren't going completely off the rails. Perhaps this time, I'd been saved.

✦

A week after the talent agency let me go, I received an email from Andrew, explaining he had moved to Charlotte to start his own company. He did not offer to represent me, and I didn't ask. He wished me the best. I replied with my congratulations. Understanding that I was at my own career crossroads, I asked him for some parting advice.

He replied, "You have to do whatever makes you happy."

This stung, because in our most recent interactions, I knew I'd come across as someone who didn't really know what would make her happy. When we first started working together, I'd been so clear and confident about my goals and what I thought I wanted to achieve.

He'd done all he could do—or was willing to do—for me. He had a vision for what taking the Memphis job could do for my career, and I didn't feel the same way. He'd tried to find me a job in Portland, but things just didn't work out. Agents only get paid if they secure the deal. He'd spent time on me, and time is money.

I tried to take Andrew's advice, though, searching my memories for a time when I was truly happy. I remembered when Shawn and I took a cruise to the Bahamas before I started my job at Channel 5. On that trip, we snorkeled and rode jet skis around the island, splashing around in the water and living the relaxing island life. My mind wasn't preoccupied, only existing in the present moment. A complete absence of stress. That was five years ago, and during vacation, so did it even count? Did I have any idea what would make me happy in my regular, everyday life? I liked writing in my journal. Did that count?

When I worked at Channel 5, I was often asked to speak at school career days. I usually began my presentation like this: "Who hates math?"

CHAPTER TWENTY-SEVEN

Half the class would raise their hands.

"Now, imagine being stuck in math class for the rest of your life!"

Groans across the room.

"Now, think about the subjects you really like. What are your hobbies? Or favorite extracurricular activities?" I'd watch their faces light up. "Now, imagine having a job like that. Imagine getting paid to do something you enjoy."

Back then, I believed that you could pick the perfect thing. But what happens when circumstances change and it shakes up all your best-laid plans and makes you question all the things you thought you wanted?

Perhaps "happy" wasn't even the right word. Perhaps a better question to ask myself was: What would bring me joy?

✦

I couldn't stop mentally reversing the clock back to our life in Charleston. In one moment, we were on the career fast-track, and in the next, I wanted to buy a house. I also felt afraid to want it. I felt guilty for wanting it. I felt like I shouldn't want it because buying the house planted a major detour on the path that Shawn and I had been taking together. Now we were on different paths, and I was trying to make sense of it.

I tried to explain this to Shawn during our weekly date to Portland City Grill. We got there early, before the happy hour crowd, and found an open table by the windows overlooking the city. Admiring the Portland skyline and enjoying a glass of pinot noir put me at ease. I had a moment of clarity. "I'm not sure I want to hop from city to city, trying to get ahead in this business. I had to move away to realize that, but I miss home. I miss our friends. I miss our life."

"I know that's how you feel. But Angie, I couldn't stay there. Not the way things were. We never saw each other. Work was a dead end. I felt like I was going crazy."

For the first time, I realized how much Shawn reminded me of Cam. I'd heard how sometimes women marry men who remind them of their dads and the notion seemed creepy. I couldn't deny the similarities. Both were dark-haired and handsome and possessed a quiet reserve. Shawn never felt the need to overly explain himself or make decisions by committee. His college fraternity brother had nicknamed him "Covert." After Shawn lost his own father, he'd developed a way of surviving in the world. He didn't mince words or play games. I'd always seen the goodness, since that first day in the television production class when I realized I was sitting a few seats away from the guy who'd invented the "Moffatt Method."

"Shawn, I understand. You needed to do this. And I wanted you to have this opportunity, I really did." I paused.

"I thought I wanted it, too. Now, I'm just confused. I want a successful career, but I don't want to give up everything else I care about in the process."

"Angie, you loved that house. I know that. I liked it, too. I wasn't attached to it like you were. It's just stuff. I don't need it."

This felt like a kick in the gut. This was the place where we could never see eye to eye. "I don't want stuff. I want a home. I want to feel content. That doesn't mean I want to settle."

"I told you I only needed a year. After this, I don't care where we go."

Where would that be? After being on the same path for so long, a path that seemed to magically roll out for us like a yellow brick road, we were, undeniably, at a split. "Shawn, it seems like we want different things."

He nodded. "Yes, I think we do."

There it was. We said it. It was out in the open. The line in the sand. The last time we were at this place, we were standing in our new house in Charleston, and he was telling me he couldn't stay in Charleston long-term. Without thinking it all the way through, I'd asked Don to switch my schedule so Shawn and I could spend more time together. Then, Shawn ended up moving 3,000 miles away. This time, I had no bright ideas about how to fix it. I didn't feel inspired to try because trying to fix things only complicated the situation.

"Well, what do you think we should do about that?" I asked. The boldness, the directness, and the possible impact of my question scared me. But I needed to know where we stood.

"I want to stay married to you," he said, clear and certain. "That's what I want." I looked away and blinked, unable to stop the single tear from spilling out and burning my cheek. I brushed it away. What if he'd said something different? "I know you haven't been in a good place, so please don't take this the wrong way," he said. "But I feel closer to you now than I ever have." I stared at him. How was that even possible? "What I mean is, I've enjoyed having you around. I love coming home from work and seeing you there. I love that I can plan a weekend getaway, and you're available to go. I know you don't feel great, but I feel like I'm finally getting to see you. All of you."

I looked out the restaurant window, meditating on the lights glistening on the mountainside. I tried to process this. I was at my worst, and he loved me even more? What he was saying, I realized, was that above all of it—the house, our successful careers, our Charleston social life—he wanted me. For better or worse. And I wanted him too.

So maybe that's how it felt. Maybe that's what it felt like to stay.

COMING ALIVE

Since, for the indefinite time being, we were still living in Portland, I decided that I needed to start living. That meant less channel surfing and boxed hair color from Walgreens and more getting out of the apartment. Shawn signed us up for a gym membership. The gym had several locations around the city, including one near Shawn's work and one a short drive from our apartment. The gym near our apartment was a renovated warehouse with an urban vibe. I had to force myself to go, but once I stepped on the treadmill and started running to the beat of my playlist, I felt better. I never left the gym in a bad mood.

Sometimes I'd see Edie, the dance instructor from the hip-hop class I took when I first got to Portland. She taught group fitness classes at the gym, and I was in awe of her ability to carry that breezy confidence with her wherever she went. She didn't seem to recognize me, so I kept my distance. I didn't want to be a weird stalker girl, but I couldn't stop watching her. To me, she had something I didn't have. I didn't know what it was, but I wanted it.

On Shawn's days off, we went to the gym together. One day, as we were side-by-side doing crunches on big inflatable exercise balls, it hit me. I can do this anywhere. How profound! Maybe I simply got caught up in the music pulsing through the overhead speakers, but the idea that I could do this anywhere felt like a revelation. There I was, forgetting to be sad. I felt present and connected to my body; I was 100 percent in the room. Perhaps that elusive thing I was seeking—the certain something about Edie, about Rita at Channel 5, about Nancy O'Dell that I was so drawn to— was inside of me too. Perhaps that confidence I craved came from discovering those parts of myself that stay with me always, that travel with me wherever I go.

✦

One day, Chris and I walked to the movies. I bought a jumbo-sized popcorn and a large Diet Coke and arranged to meet him in the lobby afterward. He went off to watch "The Recruit," and I walked into the theater showing "How to Lose a Guy in 10 Days." I'd always heard how terrible and depressing it was going to the movies alone. That was not my experience. If you laugh out loud and no one is around to hear it, did you really laugh? Was it even funny? As it turns out, it was indeed very funny. Not everything had to be shared. Some experiences could be just for me.

Over the next couple of months, I got more comfortable doing things on my own. At night, when I was home flipping channels, I'd stop to watch a dark-haired, wide-grinned Texas preacher on television. My grandmother and I used to watch "The PTL Club," a Christian program hosted by televangelists Jim and Tammy Faye Bakker. My grandmother was skeptical of their prosperity gospel. "They're just trying to get our money," she'd say. She watched the show anyway, sometimes to listen to the sermon and other times to laugh about Tammy Faye's fake eyelashes. Remembering those days, now alone in my Portland apartment, I'd sit in the folding egg chair, rest my feet on the ottoman, pop open a Killian's and watch the Texas preacher deliver his message as if it were a comedy. I thought: This guy can't be for real. I imagined that it could be great material for skits on "Saturday Night Live."

I wanted to be skeptical, but his words rang true. He talked about forgiveness and how withholding our forgiveness hurts us, too. We have the power to free ourselves from the way other people have hurt us. If we don't forgive, the offender continues to control us. I tried to get my mind around that. I'd never deliberately withheld my forgiveness, but I knew I still carried around a lot of pain. It occurred to me that forgiveness was possible, but maybe it just took time to get the job all the way done. Perhaps there was a better word: healing.

The TV preacher went on to say that there was no reason to be jealous of other people's blessings because God has enough blessings to go around. He said we all have a unique path, carved out just for us. I'd always felt like God was looking out for me, but I'd never considered the possibility of infinite blessings. Working in TV news, the blessings most certainly felt finite. There was not unlimited space at the top. But was getting to the top the only worthy goal? In the book "What Should I Do With My Life?" the author had been intrigued by people who seemed to have found their true calling. He learned that many didn't pick it; they stumbled into it, or through a series of setbacks, the mysterious so-called calling found its way to them.

I looked down at my cat, curled up in my lap. He was a stray rescued from the animal shelter, and he was always nervous and hiding; I was the only one he ever felt safe around. Lately, I'd caught him strutting around the apartment. Perhaps he'd sensed a shift in my vibe, too. I stroked his fur and listened to him purr.

✦

One Saturday night, my friend Jen called. Jen was a young attorney about my age who my mom had worked for during her short time in Portland. She told me she was headed to a country bar in a nearby town. "I'll pick you up. It will be fun."

"I don't think so," I said. "I'm not dressed. I was about to sit down and watch a movie."

I'd gotten so comfortable spending time alone that I'd begun to prefer it. Getting dressed and talking to people felt like a lot of effort. Jen had told me that she would stay in touch with me after my mom left, and she was making good on her promise.

"Oh, come on. I'm meeting up with some friends. They'd love to meet you."

I didn't have an excuse. I was sitting home alone on a Saturday night. It's not like I had an exhausting week at work and needed the R&R. I'd been resting for months. "OK, you talked me into it."

I hung up and dug through my shoebox-sized closet looking for something to wear. The great thing about country bars is that the dress code is basic. Jeans. Boots. Belt. I spent 10 minutes in front of the mirror, adding mascara and lip gloss and attempting to fluff up my hair. Good enough.

When Jen and I arrived at the bar, we found her friends, ordered some beers and made our way to a booth. I slid in first so I could hide in the corner up against the wall and nurse my beer. I'd just sit, drink and people-watch. Perfect.

"May I have this dance?" An older man stood at the end of the booth and extended his hand in my direction.

"Oh, no. No. Thank you. I'm good. No, but thanks." The longest "no" ever. But still, he didn't seem to comprehend.

"I insist," he said, in a gentlemanly honky-tonk kind of way.

"Go, Angie, go!" Jen said, sliding out the booth so I could get out.

I shot her a look as if to say, "OK, but you're dancing with him next," and I scooted out to meet my dance partner.

He grabbed my hand and led me out to the floor. "Do you know how to two-step?" he asked.

"Sort of. Not really," I said. I still couldn't figure out why, out of all the women in the bar—out of all the women wearing form-fitting Wranglers, leather boots and sexy hats—he wanted to dance with me. I was in a pair of faded Old Navy jeans, pleather Aerosole boots and a long-sleeved T-shirt from Target. My personality was certainly lacking that night as well—hardly flaunting my inner Shania.

"Just follow my lead." He pulled me in, and instantly, we were absorbed into the rhythm of the dance floor, falling in step with every other couple, following the same circle, around and around and around. Whenever I danced with Shawn, he always let me lead. At fraternity parties in college, we'd mastered some beer-buzzed version of the Carolina Shag. We were most certainly not doing it right, but we'd shuffle, step and spin and do a great job faking it. This man in the country bar knew how to do the dance and how to lead me through it. At first, I had a hard time relaxing enough to let him. It was unnerving, the trust involved.

It was also incredibly liberating, sliding around the edges of the dance floor, turning fast when we got to the corners, spinning like we were on a ride at the fair. We danced song after song, in some sort of alternate universe controlled by electric guitars and disco lights. In my mind, I saw my grandmother dancing too: at wedding receptions, in the garage on Marilyn Drive, on the sandy floor of the beach house during the only vacation my family ever took. She lit up the room. I could feel her, moving around and through me. She was there, inside that country bar. Circling, floating, spinning across the dance floor. Reminding me how it felt to be alive.

At the end of the night, the man led me back to my friends and said goodnight. I never even got his name. It's possible that he'd been an angel himself. Or, like me, he simply wanted—or needed—to dance.

DOORS

When I lost my agent, I'd let go of the quest to get work in Portland. If I'd gotten a job right away it might've been different, but now, I was—finally—learning to live in the moment. We were on the downhill stretch of our year in Portland, and after that it would be time to move on to ... who knows? The question no longer bothered me so much.

When I came home one afternoon in March and pressed play on the answering machine, it was like getting startled awake from a dream. The caller introduced himself as the news director at KATU TV, the ABC station in Portland. He'd finally looked at my resume and wanted to know if we could set up a time to meet. His voice was dry and detached, and I tensed at the sound of it. I couldn't explain it; it's not like I expected sunshine and rainbows, but the message had not a hint of warmth and I felt it in my body, a nervous anxiety. I no longer had an agent to have uncomfortable conversations on my behalf, so I called back and agreed to the interview.

Days later, the news director, a producer and I met for lunch at a restaurant near the waterfront. They were polite, but I got the sense that they weren't that into me either.

Perhaps my outward appearance was too sunshine and rainbows for them. Or maybe they sensed my trepidation.

The news director asked me, "How is our station different from the others?"

"I love your anchors," I said. "They seem so friendly, so relatable. I like the way your station delivers the news." That was true. I liked their on-air style. I wondered about the work environment behind the scenes. I talked with my hands, as I always do. I noticed them shaking and lowered them to my lap.

The news director asked when I could start. I told him that we had some good friends from Charleston coming to visit soon, so right after that. He replied, "We're about to go to war," noting American troops were poised to invade Iraq.

"Or," I said, backpedaling, "I could start right away." I knew at that moment, I'd failed the test. I was off my game. They never called back, and I was actually relieved. Weeks later, I'd watch the news as Portland residents gathered in the streets, breaking windows, vandalizing buildings—protesting the war.

When I left the restaurant that day, I considered stopping to ask the hostess for an application. I'd worked in restaurants in high school and college, so the idea wasn't out of the question. But the other big news story in Portland was unemployment. I'd seen a report about a new restaurant in another part of town. In preparation for the grand opening, applicants were lined up out the door and along the sidewalk. The reporter interviewed people vying for jobs, many with upper-level degrees. I walked out of the restaurant without picking up an application.

Shortly after that, I heard about a part-time writer position at Shawn's station, and I had a completely different reaction. It seemed like the perfect scenario: no contracts, and I could enjoy the fast-paced energy of the newsroom, instead of traipsing around town with a microphone in the rain. And I'd get to write.

If I got this job, maybe we'd stay in Portland longer than we thought. Maybe we'd like that. During the interview, as the executive producer surveyed my resume, I tried to convince her that I understood the job description. I didn't have a secret plan to wiggle my way into an on-air position. She left me sitting at a computer in a quiet room to produce some writing samples.

A couple of weeks later, inside a dark bar with too-loud music, Chris leaned over and shouted in my ear, "They went with the other girl. They said you were both good, but in the end, they liked her writing style better." He wasn't trying to hurt my feelings; he was just being frank. Working in news, we'd grown accustomed to giving it to each other straight. Everybody talked; there were no secrets. If Chris hadn't told me why I didn't get the job, I would've forced it out of

Shawn. But just because I wanted to know, it didn't stop the burning sensation in my chest.

"Oh," was all I could say. My college professor had told me I could build a career around my writing ability. Writing had become my solace in Portland, and to have it rejected felt like too much. The music shook my eardrums. I tried to breathe, not sure whether I might pass out or cry.

✦

Much like flowers and the real estate market, apparently job opportunities came alive in the springtime too. In April, while having lunch at a brewery downtown, Shawn told me that the ABC station in Charleston was looking for a main anchor. "You should apply for that," he said.

"Really?" I asked. "You'd be willing to move back to Charleston?" My stomach did a little flip.

"For this, yes. It's a main anchor position. You'd be great."

I fantasized about seeing my face on a billboard on I-26. All the stations put their main anchors on billboards. I saw myself being a leader in the newsroom and going out in the community, speaking at public events. After the year I'd had, I would return to Charleston with a new perspective. I would have so much energy and a positive attitude. I'd appreciate everything.

I reached out to the news director and flew home for the interview. After the set test, the news director asked me, "You worked at Channel 5. So why do you want to work here?"

This station was last place in the ratings, and I thought coming from Channel 5 would give me an advantage. The plan backfired. He seemed suspicious. The undertone of his question: "Why would you want to be number three when you were once number one?"

"Because I know Charleston," I said. "And, honestly, I'd love to come back. I have the experience and the credibility to be a main anchor. I know I'd do a good job." I wanted this job, and I hoped I didn't sound as desperate as I now felt. But his question stayed with me: Why do you want to do this?

He told me he'd call, but he never did.

✦

In June, Shawn and I celebrated our third year of marriage. Shawn's mom and sister traveled to Portland, and they stayed at our apartment and played tourist while Shawn and I spent the weekend in a downtown hotel. When we returned, they greeted us with stories about their adventures. They'd spent most of their time exploring Washington Park in the west hills. There, they visited the Oregon Zoo, the arboretum, the Japanese garden and the famous rose garden overlooking the Portland skyline. They stuffed our refrigerator with fresh soup, sandwiches and sweet treats from Elephants Delicatessen. They packed more activities into a few days than I'd done in eight months. This felt like a revelation. I'd once imagined that living in Portland would feel like an extended vacation, a retreat. But it never did; I'd been too consumed with loss. I'd missed an opportunity, but I told myself I still had time to make up for it.

At the end of their visit, Shawn's sister set a black-and-white photo on the kitchen counter, an ultrasound, surprising us with the news that she was pregnant. Shawn was going to be an uncle. After his dad died when Shawn and his sister were still young, the two of them and their mom had developed an independence, a do-your-own-thing attitude. Given my emotional attachments to my own family, I never fully understood this about them. The shadowy photo of his unborn nephew shifted something in Shawn. It was as if he'd realized for the first time: His family was 3,000 miles away too. He wanted to know his sister's child, and for his nephew to know him.

After their visit, Shawn and I shopped at Elephants, drove to Washington Park and enjoyed a picnic by the roses. Still, I sensed that our time in Portland was, indeed, ending. Despite how difficult the past year had been, I'd remember it fondly.

✦

"We could keep moving around from city to city, but for what?" Shawn asked a month later during a home-cooked candlelight dinner. "I guess it depends on what we're really working toward." I'd been stumbling around with these questions since before we ever left Charleston, but they'd never entered Shawn's mind until now.

"I don't know anymore," I said, sticking my nose in a glass of Blue Moon pinot noir. Lately, my favorite pastime was browsing Fred Meyer, seeking new wines to try and ingredients for my latest recipe. It was oddly fulfilling. "I had no idea I'd end up here. Not just here in Portland, but here in life." Thinking back to my recent unsuccessful job interviews and how they'd made me second-guess myself, I said, "I'm terrified to make another choice, knowing how a simple decision can alter my course so dramatically."

"I've never approached my life that way," he said. "If a door closes, I don't question it. I may not like it, but I assume it happened for a reason. I look for the next opportunity."

"Why is that?" I asked.

"That's just how I am. Doors open. Doors close. It's as simple as that."

All this time, I thought a closing door meant I'd done something wrong. For the past year, as my personal and professional life unraveled, I believed I'd caused it somehow.

I considered my choices—my flip-flopping changes of heart—over and over. Other times, I'd pointed a finger at Shawn's choices, insinuating it was his fault for wanting different things, for taking the job in Portland.

For the first time, I saw how wrong—and how mixed up—I was about success and failure, and perhaps life in general. I'd believed that I needed to do all the right things, in the right order. I believed that doing it right was the key to opening doors, and very specific doors at that. If things didn't work out the way I'd hoped, and the way I'd planned, then I'd failed. And failure was a scary thing. I'd created a story—an image—in my mind about how my life would unfold. If my life never lived up to the image and the story never came true, then what would that say about me? Who would I be then?

I'd been reading the book I borrowed from the library, "The Mystery of God's Will." The author said some of life's biggest questions don't have concrete answers. We'd discussed God's will in my church youth group back in high school too. If we believed that God had a plan, then what about free will? Were we screwing up the plan with all our dumb decisions? Or was our freedom to choose all part of the plan? We never solved it.

"Have you ever thought about trying again for law school?" I asked.

"No. I studied my ass off for the LSAT and I know if I took it again, I wouldn't score much higher. Besides, I was always good at TV and realized I was just resisting the inevitable. I never really wanted to practice law. I probably would've done something in entertainment. Maybe I would've become an agent or something."

"You could've been my agent," I said, smiling. In the early days of my career, when my pager went off—which usually meant breaking news and my cue to go in to work—Shawn would be the first to jump off the couch, go to my closet, pull an outfit together and start packing my bag if the story required me to work overnight or head out of town. He'd assumed the role of my personal fashion consultant, breaking it to me not-so-gently that my suits—the ones I bought at Dress Barn—were too big. He also convinced me to toss half the shoes in my closet. If it weren't for Shawn, I'd still be trapped in the 1980s, teasing my bangs and wearing Keds.

He'd always done what he could to help me succeed. He didn't see me as a failure. Portland had simply presented a lot of closed doors. One door had opened for me here: the doorway to myself. Portland opened my mind; it changed my perspective in ways I'd never forget.

We finished dinner in our 400-square-foot apartment, sitting on the wooden bar stools I bought from Target. A song by Hootie and the Blowfish spun memories of college days.

"Well," I said, raising my glass. "Here's to open doors."

✦

Another month passed and Shawn's year in Portland was almost up. That's when the door to go back home to Charleston flew open. It started when Don from Channel 5 sent Shawn an email. He wrote, "I'm looking for a good director. Know any?"

Shawn printed the message and brought it home from work. "Hey, look at this," he said, standing over me while I processed the note. "What do you think?"

My heart fluttered. If this was going to happen, we needed to do it right. "I think you need to talk to Don. He seems to be asking you, honestly, if you know of any good directors to recommend. He may also be feeling you out, wondering if that good director is you. You need to call him. Find out if this opening is right for you. You have to decide if going back is worth it to you."

Shawn called Don the next day and said he did know of someone. He was, indeed, the good director. Don was happy to hear this and offered Shawn a promotion, inviting him to come back to Channel 5 and manage the entire production department. The salary would be higher, comparable to what he was making in Portland. That's why Shawn believed taking the job in Portland was necessary. It gave him leverage. If he'd stayed in Charleston, he might still be waiting.

Shawn and I met for lunch on the waterfront so he could tell me all about it. This felt too good to be true. It would only be a matter of time before Don offered me a position too. A reporter, perhaps. Part-time, maybe, depending on whether they had openings. I wouldn't care because all I needed was to get my foot back in the door. Things were falling back into place, I thought, just like they used to.

I got ahead of myself.

"There's one thing," Shawn said. "If I take this job, you won't be able to work there. Corporate is cracking down on its nepotism policy. Don said it was OK that we got married while we were already working at the station. But they won't hire both of us back."

I felt the ground shift. I thought I might vomit right there in the middle of our nice lunch on the waterfront. This never, ever occurred to me, that being married was now a conflict of interest. Our days of being a package deal were officially over. It was an ironic twist of fate.

Shawn was sympathetic—to a degree. He seemed relatively unfazed. "This might be a good thing for you," Shawn said. "A chance to explore other things."

I'd read "What Should I Do With My Life?" from cover to cover. We'd just had a conversation about open and closed doors, and I'd raised my glass and said a freaking toast. But there I was, still thinking things would work out just how I planned them in my mind. "Well, this just sucks," is what I finally said out loud. "It's not fair." Still, I wanted him to take the job. Shawn was my ticket home.

PART THREE

BEGIN AGAIN

Sometimes, transitions are invisible; changes happen slowly over time until one day you look around and wonder—how did I get here?

Moving is different. The before and after happens before your eyes.

I called the moving company that Mom had hired when she moved back to Charleston. I took mental snapshots along the way, as we stripped our tiny tree house apartment bare. I was now ready to go. But I also didn't want to rush through the ending.

About a week before we left, I got a call from my friend Meredith, who anchored the morning show at Channel 2 in Charleston—the position once held by Nancy O'Dell. We became friends when I anchored the morning show at Channel 5, after I emailed her in search of a hairdresser.

"Guess what?" she said. "I told my news director you were moving back and his eyes got wide and he said, 'She is? Tell her I'd like to talk to her.'"

"Really? He sounded interested?"

"Yeah, he did. But there's no rush. I told him you were in the process of moving. Just give him a call when you get here."

Meredith had recently accepted an anchor job in Dallas. The new morning show anchor had already been selected, so applying to work at Channel 2 hadn't occurred to me. After we hung up, I sat down on the sofa in our apartment surrounded by boxes, contemplating how life had led me full circle. I didn't know what to make of it. I decided not to think about it until we got back to Charleston.

✦

On our last day in Portland, the movers loaded up our belongings. That night, we slept on an air mattress in the empty apartment. The following morning, we packed the car with our few remaining things, and put my cat in the carrier in the back seat. Shawn drove out of the resident parking garage and parked on the street in front of the building so I could return the key to the management office. On the way out, I stood on the top brick step overlooking the tree-lined road, the sun peeking through. The light reflected off the pavement, a kaleidoscope of black and silver. I took a panoramic picture in my mind and said, "Goodbye, Portland." As I climbed into the passenger seat of our black Hyundai, I felt the ease of the lighter load, how it felt to move forward without a heavy weight in tow.

Shawn and I traveled from Portland to Reno and down to Las Vegas. I'd never been to Vegas. Shawn had found an affordable rate at a hotel at the end of the strip that looked like it was made of gold. We relaxed by the wave pool, and when I wanted a drink, all I had to do was raise the little white flag on my lounge chair to beckon the waiter. Just like that, our year in Portland felt like another lifetime.

Back on the road, when the view was nothing but desert and horizon, I pulled out my journal and scribbled thoughts as they came to me. Past and present blurred together. I now understood that people change, circumstances change and the best-laid plans come undone. Lessons circle back around until you learn them.

I looked over at Shawn—eyes on the road, forward focused, as always. I wasn't the woman he married, at least not from the outside looking in. The young TV news anchor with Hollywood dreams. We'd made so many plans around these dreams. Through it all, he had not said goodbye. He was still here.

Still holding my pen and my notebook, I decided to interview him. "What's the biggest thing you've learned this year?"

He didn't hesitate. "You're either running away from something. Or you're running to something." I realized that I'd spent my life doing both—running away from pain and sadness and running toward the picture of happiness I'd created in my mind. I set down my pen, stared out the window and looked to where the desert met the horizon, taking in the infinite open space. Shawn looked over and asked, "Have you ever thought about writing a book?"

"I don't know." I considered the question. "Maybe."

Driving back home to Charleston from Portland, I realized I was living a story I would tell one day. But I sensed I was still in the middle of it. I'd learned something important during my time away from the spotlight, away from everything I'd built my identity around. But I didn't know what would come of it. I was still learning. There were still miles yet to go.

✦

Mom and Patrick had recently reconciled. Their reunion happened slowly, and they finally came to terms with the issues that had driven them apart. Mom said, simply put, they got back together because they stopped being angry.

Mom moved back in with Patrick, and Shawn and I moved into her two-bedroom apartment and took over the lease. After Shawn and I had been back in Charleston for a few days, I called the news director at Channel 2.

"Meredith told me to give you a call," I said, breaking the ice. We scheduled a meeting for the next day.

I dressed in my pressed navy suit and drove across the Cooper River and coasted down the Ravenel Bridge into Mount Pleasant. As I approached the traffic light, I admired the two-story brick building on my left, complete with a pond, a large fountain, and important-looking satellite dishes speckled about the lawn. I fixated on the call letters WCBD TV.

The news director, Greg, a big, friendly-looking man, greeted me in the lobby. Channel 2 boasted a brand-new, hurricane-proof building, full of high-tech toys and its own industrial-sized Keurig coffeemaker in the break room. It was a new addition and Greg seemed quite proud of it. I was impressed by the dozens and dozens of K-Cups and all the flavors. I chose French vanilla and watched in awe as it brewed a perfect, single cup. They even had flavored creamer.

Greg made a cup for himself and led me on a tour around the building. He dazzled me with plans to beat the competition—the historically unbeatable Channel 5—and explained how he wanted me to be a part of the team. He painted exciting scenarios that involved me stopping at Starbucks to pick up coffee for insiders at the mayor's office and the police department, spending the morning in their offices and gathering leads. He wanted in-depth. He wanted stories that mattered. I smiled, nodded and placed myself in the center of his vision. I got swept up.

When the interview was over, I glided out of the building. As I drove back over the bridge, I turned up the radio. I'm back, I thought.

The next day Greg called me at precisely the time he said he would. "I'd like to offer you the position of senior reporter," he said. There were no anchor positions available at the moment, but I perked up at the word "senior" in front of "reporter." I knew the pay was going to be good. "The pay is $30,000 and you'll get a $1,000 a year clothing allowance."

I tried to mask my disappointment. This was less than what I'd been making at Channel 5, and I had more experience than the other reporters at the station. "OK, that's great. Thank you. But do you think we can talk about the pay?"

"I can tell you that you'll be the highest-paid reporter here." I noted the subtle shift in his tone. "Let me know if you're interested or if you're not, so I can move on to the next candidate."

This was not the first time I'd been offered a salary lower than what I'd hoped for. In the early years of my career, I'd been so eager to get my foot in the door that I'd accept the position and bet on my ability to work my way up. But this interaction felt different. It wasn't about the money, not entirely. It was about how quickly he made it known that I was replaceable. Plus, I wanted those other jobs more than I wanted this. I should've said "thanks but no thanks" right then and there. But I second-guessed that impulse and told myself that I wasn't in a situation to negotiate. He gave me 24 hours to decide.

"Sure. I understand," I said, "I'll think about it and let you know something tomorrow."

The thing I was certain about: my heart was somewhere else—Channel 5. I hung up and immediately dialed Don's number. I told him that Channel 2 had just offered me a job, and I wasn't going to take it if there was any chance that I could come back. He told me to hang tight. He said he was going to walk down and talk to Rita. An hour later, he called back and said, "You should probably take that job."

Of all the doors that had closed in my career, this one hurt the most.

The next day, as I held the pen, surrounded by a smiling Greg, the general manager and the human resources director at Channel 2, I watched the events of the last year flash before me: buying the house, turning down Memphis, selling the house, moving to Portland and back, and a series of dead-end job interviews.

If I didn't sign the contract, what else would I do? I wasn't ready for my career to end, not like this. I'd invested so much time; I'd worked so hard. I signed my name because I believed I didn't have a choice. I signed my name and silenced the internal alarm bells. Despite Rita's advice before I moved to Portland, I didn't listen to my heart, not this time. I didn't trust what my heart had to say.

CLOCKS

My doubts were intercepted by the fanfare surrounding my return. The Post and Courier published an article welcoming me back to Charleston TV. In the article, Greg referred to me as "a skilled and experienced newswoman" and "a natural." I noted all the things about the work that came somewhat easily for me: writing, communicating, telling stories and the ability to talk to the camera in a personable way. My confident on-air persona was the result of years of practice and daily preparation, and for a moment I forgot about all the times when it didn't feel so natural, like pushing a boulder uphill. I'd soon be reminded.

Several days before I was scheduled to start my new job as senior reporter at Channel 2, Greg called. He wanted to know if I was available the next day to do a series of live shots for the morning show during a blood drive sponsored by the television station. Since my contract had not officially begun, he said he would hire me for the day as a freelancer. "It'll be a chance to show you off to the competition," he said.

After nine months of drinking Portland micro brews and indulging in late-night bar food, I squeezed into a skirt and jacket and reported to the event hall hosting the blood drive.

I said hello to the morning anchors for the first time, live on the air. I knew them; I knew almost everyone in Charleston TV. Our chitchat was friendly and light-hearted, and just like that, it all came back to me, as if I'd done it yesterday.

Two days later, on my first official day at work, Greg asked me to stick around the building and learn the computer system. About an hour after the morning meeting, the newsroom fell silent as we turned our attention to the commotion on the police scanner. "It sounds like a bank robbery in West Ashley," a producer shouted. She looked around the room. All the reporters were out. Greg emerged from his office.

"Angie, can you go?" he asked.

"Sure," I said, hopping up from my desk and grabbing my briefcase. "Where are we going?"

"It's on Highway 61 near Old Towne Road. The bank across from the drug store," the assignment editor said. "Go with Jimmy."

On the way out the door, the producer asked, "Can you do a live shot for noon?"

"Yes," I said. "No problem."

It was 10:30. I rarely missed a deadline. Back in my morning show days, it wasn't uncommon to run down the hall to the set with less than a minute on the clock. I'd clip on my microphone, quickly check my scripts, one last fluff of the hair, and live in three, two, one.

At this point I was on autopilot, operating on adrenaline. Jimmy and I hopped in the live truck, quickly introduced ourselves, and were on our way, breaking the speed limit. When we arrived, Jimmy got video of police working the crime scene and the yellow tape surrounding the bank building. I talked to investigators and questioned eye-witnesses. I called Jimmy over to record interviews.

We ran back to the live truck. Jimmy raised the mast, called the station to make sure they had our signal, and began rolling out cables. I listened to the interviews, wrote my script, called the producer, fed the video back to the station, put on makeup and coated my hair with a few sprays of aerosol.

With minutes to spare, I took my position in front of the camera, next to my friends, a reporter and videographer from Channel 5. We exchanged bear hugs. For a moment, it felt good to be back, to be welcomed by my friends in the business. I'd missed them, and they'd missed me. In the next moment, reality settled in. The Live 5 News Team wasn't my team anymore; it was my competition. I adjusted my earpiece, the producer said "standby," and I was live. At 12:02, it was over. It was time to turn the story into an in-depth package for the 5 and 6 p.m. shows. There had been a string of bank robberies in the area. Was there a connection?

The ticking of the clock toward the next deadline kept me going. It didn't allow me to think of anything else.

After the first few days of getting acquainted at Channel 2, I moved to the evening shift as planned. This allowed me to report for the 5, 6, and 11 p.m. newscasts and kept me on the move. I lived on Diet Cokes, frozen veggie burgers that I heated up in the break room microwave, and cans of meal replacement shakes. Within two weeks, my suits were no longer too tight. Then, they were loose. Shawn and I were back on opposite schedules, which before Portland was a way of life. Now, after months of being unemployed and idle, it seemed like we'd gone from one extreme to the other.

✦

Throughout my career, I'd spent a great deal of time teaching myself how to be conversational and relaxed in front of the camera. I loved telling stories and talking to people. But here's the thing I never learned how to do: Turn off my emotions when bad things happened.

When a producer would shout "Shhh!" and turn up the police scanner to hear what was going on, I wanted to flee the newsroom or duck under my desk. I didn't get the rush of excitement that good reporters were supposed to feel when they were assigned to breaking news stories. Breaking news was, almost 100 percent of the time, bad news.

At Channel 5, once I was promoted to morning anchor, I was shielded from some of this because I was often assigned stories I could finish in the early afternoon and was rarely called back to work for murders, fatal car wrecks, fires. I got a pass because I had to wake up at 3:30 in the morning. Plus, I was a general assignment reporter, not a beat reporter. I got to cover a little bit of everything: bad news, good news, feature stories, community issues. There was a certain relief in getting to mix it up. But at Channel 2, on the night shift, reporting bad news was a regular occurrence.

Late one night about a month after I started work, a small commuter jet went down in the woods somewhere in Berkeley County. I'd just finished my report for the 11 p.m. news and was collecting my things to leave. My heart sank. I'd didn't want to rush to the scene of a tragedy, especially in the middle of the night. I wanted to go home.

The videographer and I drove to the scene 45 minutes away. We traveled down the dark tree-lined road in search of the command center. By this time, I'd snapped into work mode. I gathered information from officials and set up to go live. Reporters from other stations lined up beside me, in front of their respective cameras. The coroner and rescue officials worked the row of microphones, and we all got our story.

The wreckage was deep in the forest, and officials said we couldn't go back until morning. It was too dark and wasn't worth the risk. The producer called Greg at home, and I waited as they decided what they wanted me to do. Should I stay in Berkeley County all night and report for the morning show? Should they call another reporter to relieve me? This went on for a while. Finally, officials decided to shut down the command center until daylight, and Greg agreed to let me come back. I went back to the station and prepared the limited information and video for the morning show. I wrote my script and left the tape on the assignment editor's desk. Once again, I collected my things to go home. In the car, the digital clock blinked 4 a.m.

I heard my wise voice rise up from within, and she wasn't as gentle. She asked: What are you doing? What have you done?

People were dead. Somewhere, family and friends were grieving the loss. I couldn't stop feeling sick over it. And I couldn't stop staring at the lights on the clock. I'd committed to three years. It felt like a sentence. I'd given my own time away, days of my own life. I had knowingly put myself in a situation I didn't want and signed my name on the dotted line.

✦

One day, I called my childhood friend Meg and set up a time to meet for lunch. I'd planned to confess to her about how I'd been living with a low-key but constant sense of dread. She'd know just what to say. Over deli sandwiches one afternoon before I reported to work, I told her that I thought I'd made a mistake.

"I don't know if I feel this way because I haven't worked in a while," I said. "Should I just suck it up and give it more time? Or is my gut telling me I'm not supposed to do this anymore?"

"Well," Meg began, carefully considering the question. "The answer could really be either, Ang. I don't think there's a right or wrong for this one. The answer is whatever you decide it is."

I thought back to dozens of stories I'd read in the book, "What Should I Do With My Life?" The personal accounts of arriving at a crossroads had opened my mind to so many possibilities. I had a strong resume and many professional contacts and connections in Charleston. But instead of daring to do something new, I'd signed the contract because I didn't want to face an unknown future once again. That, it seemed, was my biggest mistake.

✦

The following month, in October, Shawn and I traveled to New York for Don and Stephanie's wedding. It was hard to believe how much my life had changed since the day Stephanie had called me in Portland and asked me to be a bridesmaid. That day, she'd told me to relax, because I'd soon be back at work and missing the days I could stay home in my pajamas. How ironic it felt now.

At the reception, a sit-down dinner, Shawn and I joined the table reserved for guests from Channel 5. Rita sat next to me. I still felt the sting of not being allowed to come back to work for Channel 5, but she seemed happy to see me, which was disarming.

"How do you like working at Channel 2?" she asked.

"Actually," I paused. "I don't. It's just a different world over there. The work feels all-consuming and the stress is getting to me."

"It's hard," she said, and she seemed to be considering her own success and the struggles that came along with it. "Now, when I'm with my grandbaby, everything else turns off. No one has access to me when I'm with her."

I knew that's what I lacked. The ability to turn it off. I was either at work, being unexpectedly called in to work or thinking about work. Work had always preoccupied my mind. And now, it was sucking the life out of me.

Before Shawn and I left for New York, I reached out to my friend Michele, who, after getting started with fashion design in Savannah, had moved to New York to design underwear for Calvin Klein. Michele had recently married Ed, another one of our childhood friends, who was an investment banker on Wall Street.

The day after Don and Stephanie's wedding, Shawn and I met Michele and Ed for dinner. They gave us a taste of the local flavor, taking us to their favorite hangouts in their Lower East side neighborhood. Spending time with them was therapeutic because they knew me long before the TV days. They thought my job was cool, but they didn't really care one way or the other. To them, I was the same old Angie.

Michele had been recently diagnosed with cervical cancer and was undergoing treatment. The thought of losing Michele had rattled me deeply. When Shawn and Ed were absorbed in conversation, Michele confessed she didn't love city life as much as Ed did.

"I want my horses. I want to move to Montana," she said. Michele had family in Montana. She wanted to live on a ranch.

"I remember that presentation you did in eighth grade, when you told the class you like horses better than you like people," I said, laughing.

"I do like horses better," she said. "But Ed would never do it. So, I'm trying to convince him to consider Brooklyn."

In high school, Michele was known for being perpetually late; friends would honk in her driveway while she was inside drying her hair. She'd always gone at her own pace, and we loved her for who she was. She was still the same person who craved a slower life in a fast-paced world.

Years later, Ed and Michele would get divorced, and she'd echo what she had told me that night at the bar. City life wasn't a fit. The cancer had changed her.

"Life's too short," she said.

WEIGHT OF THE WORLD

One afternoon in November, I sat at my desk prepping for the county council meeting later that evening. The 5 p.m. newscast had started, and the newsroom was quiet. Our assignment editor, Susan, was at the main desk, staring at a row of monitors, watching all three local newscasts simultaneously.

"Holy shit! Holy shit! HOLY SHIT!" she said, her voice escalating from a stunned whisper to a panicked shout. She leaned on the desk, hovered over the monitor turned to Channel 5 and picked up the phone.

I looked up at the row of televisions mounted to the wall and saw the black-and-white surveillance video. Police had stormed the main hallway of a local high school, guns drawn. They ordered students to get down. Dogs on leashes sniffed around lockers and backpacks. Holy shit.

I had spent an hour each afternoon calling every police agency in three counties. I'd built relationships with the important public information officers. I had cop friends. But not one of them picked up the phone to call me with the tip. Why didn't we know about this? I suspected a viewer— probably a parent from the school—had called Channel 5.

That was one advantage of being the No. 1 station. When I worked there, viewers called the newsroom with tips all the time. Some didn't realize I'd left town and come back. Even when I held a microphone advertising the NBC logo and big number "2," people would lean out of car windows and shout, "Hey! Live 5 News!" To some, Channel 5 was the only station in town, and now I was on the outside looking in.

Susan worked the phones from the assignment desk, calling the police, I'm sure, to yell at them for not letting us know about the drug raid, and to beg them for an interview. More importantly, we needed that video! I called Pam Bailey, the public information officer for the Berkeley County School District. It was after hours, so I left a voicemail and sent a message to her digital pager. I flipped through the phone book and searched for George McCrackin, the principal of Stratford High. I left a message on someone's home answering machine, although I'm not sure who I called, exactly. I paced. I prayed. I was about to call a videographer and drive to the high school when Susan shouted across the room, "Angie, Pam Bailey's on line one!"

"Thank God," I said, grabbing the line. Pam said Mr. McCrackin was waiting at the high school and would talk to us and give us the video if we came right now. I exhaled. By 11 p.m., all of this would be resolved. We missed the story, but we were getting it now. By tomorrow, everyone would be talking about it, and it wouldn't matter who was first.

The next afternoon, when I arrived at work, Greg called me into his office. I thought he wanted to tell me, "Good job. Way to hustle. Thanks for pulling it together." But the look on his face told me he wasn't pleased. Greg scolded me for not getting reaction from students and parents. By 11 p.m., the other stations had the reaction. He said one of the day shift reporters had to go out that morning to get reaction, and we'd have it for the 5 p.m. show. "We're still behind," he said. "We're still playing catch-up on the biggest story of the year."

He had a point. I knew better than to get a one-sided story. I typically pushed the boundaries of deadlines to go the extra mile. Instead, I'd run out of time. I'd been so focused on getting the video and the interview with the principal, I dropped the ball. Perhaps, because I'd come from the historically unbeatable Channel 5, he expected more from me. But at Channel 5, a story like this would get team coverage. Don would've stayed after hours or phoned the newsroom from home and started calling the shots. Expectations would've been made known. After years in the business, I was used to getting pushed out of my comfort zone, but in that moment, I'd reached my limit.

I got up, walked out and beckoned for my photographer. "Are you ready?" I asked.

We got in the news truck and left the station. It was a sunny, crisp fall day, and we were on our way to cover the opening of the Coastal Carolina Fair, which didn't feel unusual to me—covering high school drug raids one day and amusement parks the next.

"How do you get ready for work?" the videographer asked.

"What do you mean? I take a shower, put on my suit ..."

"I mean, what are you doing to relax? Girl, you need to burn some incense or something."

I knew I was stressed. It didn't occur to me that it was so obvious.

The next day, on Friday, the high school drug raid story had made national news. MSNBC wanted the story, and their producers were talking to our producers. When I got to work, I was assigned to do a question-and-answer session with Dan Abrams during his show, "The Abrams Report." In addition to the segment, I had to cover an afternoon press conference at the police station and interview parents in the stands at the high school football game.

Before the press conference started, Greg called me from the newsroom. He told me that the MSNBC assignment should not deter me from getting the story for our own newscast. "I expect you to win at 11," he said. I should've been thrilled to be on national news, but Greg got in my head.

I was 28 years old and had been building this career for nearly a decade. I'd reported on everything from hurricanes, to crime, to politics, to the mechanical bull rides at the local fair. But this was a first. In a few moments, I would appear on national television. MSNBC. The freaking network. This was an opportunity young reporters dreamed about. This exposure could leverage my career. But something else was going through my mind: I don't want to be here.

Standing in the grass just outside the Stratford High School football stadium, I gripped the microphone and tried not to fidget in front of the camera. I gazed into the lens and breathed in, slowly. I exhaled and planted my feet, grounding myself to the earth. Bright lights illuminated the spot where I stood, creating a "look at me!" neon sign effect. I appeared poised and ready, but I wanted to run.

It was a cool, crisp Friday night in November—a perfect night for a high school football game. Through the chain-link fence, the roars of the crowd and the beat of the band amplified the feeling of unity and celebration, contrasting with the controversy that brought us there with the camera and big satellite truck.

"Stand by," the producer commanded. I pressed the plastic earpiece with my index finger, pushing it closer to my brain, amplifying the volume. In my peripheral vision I watched the small television monitor positioned on the ground by the camera. Dan Abrams narrated the scene: Two days ago, police raided the school's main hallway. They stormed in with guns drawn and ordered students to get down as drug-sniffing dogs nosed around lockers and poked backpacks. Surveillance video captured the dramatic scene, and when angry parents started calling the local news stations, the principal released the video to the media.

Then, I saw my face—right next to Dan's—in the double box. Here we go.

"Angie Mizzell joins us live from Goose Creek, South Carolina," Dan said with authority. At the sound of my own name coming out of his mouth, I swallowed, hard.

He asked all the questions I expected him to ask— "Why the guns?" "Did police use excessive force?" "What if students had been hurt, or worse?" I told him that the principal had received a tip that drugs were on campus. Police said they followed protocol. Parents were angry; drugs were never found. They accused police of overreacting and using excessive force.

Nothing I said felt like answers.

The interview lasted two minutes. When the producer gave the all-clear, I set down the microphone, bumped fists with Jimmy and walked to the satellite truck. I hoisted myself into the passenger seat, and the weight of my body melted into the vinyl. I picked up the phone to call Shawn.

When Shawn answered, I didn't tell him how I was feeling. Instead, I said, "Hey, did you see it? How was it?"

"You did great!" he said.

"I did the nervous swallow. Could you tell? I haven't done that in years."

"No, you looked good," he reassured. But months later he would tell me that was the moment that he knew: I was done. Done working at Channel 2. Done with this career.

I looked at the clock. Always on a deadline. I told Shawn goodbye and stepped out of the news truck to find Jimmy rolling up cables. The football game was over, and soon, the lights would go out, leaving us standing in the dark. Jimmy packed up the gear and suggested we drive around to the front of the school to do our report for our 11 p.m. newscast. After he set up the camera and the lights and reestablished our signal, he pulled out a Marlboro Red. I asked for one, explaining that I didn't really smoke. Which was what I always said when I bummed a cigarette.

I stared at the stars, not caring about how in 15 minutes I'd be live on camera once again. This close to airtime, I typically touched up my makeup, looked over my notes, and mentally prepared to be "on" again. But I'd used up all my adrenaline during my two minutes on national television. I had none left. I inhaled the cigarette, savoring the tiny explosion in my lungs. It gave me a buzz. This small rebellion made me feel calm and centered, and that felt new. I lingered in that place for a while. A few minutes before airtime, I grabbed my notes and took my position in front of the camera.

CYCLES

Perhaps from Greg's perspective, our interactions played out differently. Or perhaps he just moved on, because soon, he promoted me to crime reporter. Even though covering crime often made me feel sick, I'd now become a robot. I accepted the promotion, not certain if I had a choice in the matter anyway. I moved to the day shift. The main anchor, Darla, and I had our own commercial. The marketing team shot the commercial at night in the station parking lot, with special lighting to make it look like we were at a crime scene. Together, Darla and I were the News 2 Crime Trackers. That part, making the commercial, was fun.

I'd met Darla a couple of years earlier when I was covering a felony DUI sentencing for Channel 5. We sat side by side in the courtroom as the mother of the young girl killed in the crash expressed her grief to the judge. The judge listened with tears in his eyes. Darla and I choked back sobs, trying desperately to not draw attention. I tried to compartmentalize, but it was impossible not to feel this mother's anguish and despair as she held up pictures of her teenaged daughter. I thought about my own mom and imagined her pain if something like that ever happened to me. It was comforting to have Darla next to me, sharing the human experience.

Darla returned from maternity leave a month after I started working at Channel 2. We'd only interacted that one time when we covered the DUI story, but her down-to-earth nature made me feel like I'd known her forever. She quickly became my confidant, mainly because we always found ourselves in the makeup room at the same time before the newscast. We were both in a period of transition. While I was trying to reestablish my life in Charleston, Darla was trying to figure out how to be the 5, 6 and 11 p.m. anchor and the mother of infant twins.

Each afternoon Darla arrived in the newsroom, always professional, but often looking tired and sometimes unsettled. One day, she sat down at her desk in tears because one of her babies was sick. Her voice cracked when she told me how he held out his arms and said, "Ma-ma-ma," as she walked out the door.

Her main anchor job had looked so glamorous to me, but I saw her struggle. My life felt incredibly out of balance, and I didn't have kids. One day in the makeup room, I told Darla how unhappy I felt. "I'm trying so hard to make this work, but it just feels so wrong. I can't imagine working here for the next three years. But what can I do? I signed a contract."

She thought for a moment, seriously pondering the question, like she might have considered the same thing herself.

"My dad always says choices are just choices. You make one and the consequences will be what they're going to be. If you don't like the outcome, you make another choice."

I'd been internally beating myself up for taking this job and ignoring the sirens going off in my body. Darla's advice normalized my situation and quieted the drama. I'd made a choice for reasons that made sense to me at the time. I didn't like the outcome, but I wasn't ready to make a new choice. At that moment, just admitting that I didn't like my job, without shame, was enough. I gave myself permission to stop pretending. I gave myself permission to feel the way I felt.

Darla's co-anchor, Carolyn, sat next to us in the newsroom. Carolyn and I had worked together at Channel 5; she was one of the local celebrities I'd grown up watching. She'd left Charleston for a stint in Chicago before moving back to town and taking a main anchor position at Channel 2.

Carolyn was muscular, glowing and crack-you-up funny. One day, as she sat at her desk snacking on a sweet potato, she tilted her head my way and said, "Girl, you're looking good." She stared at me for another second, sizing me up. "Sexy."

I laughed and said thank you, accepting the compliment. We continued to work, banging out scripts for the upcoming newscast. Now, approaching 30, I'd noticed that I seemed to be growing into myself. I'd finally perfected that long-layered, just below the shoulder TV hair that Charleston anchors were known for. My hairdresser, Randall, had been so inspired by Darla's look that he'd convinced me to "go blonde"—really blonde—and the look was working for me. Long gone were the days of feeling timid to pick up the phone, interrupt someone's day and ask for an interview. I knew that when I said my name, the caller would recognize it and most likely agree to whatever I needed to get my story on the air by news time.

There was the irony: As my job continued to get easier because I'd become so good at it, it felt harder.

✦

In the months that followed, I lived on the up-and-down roller coaster of good days and bad days, all depending on the type of story I'd covered. I let go of my dream of becoming the next Nancy O'Dell. Part of me still believed it would be totally wonderful if that somehow, miraculously, worked out. But I didn't think about it as much anymore, and I didn't consider getting another agent.

I loved the apartment community where Shawn and I lived. The grounds were beautifully landscaped with flowers and palm trees and the roads were lined with sidewalks.

Still, I missed our house, and I regretted letting go of it. If I had known we'd be back in Charleston so soon, perhaps we could've figured out a way to hold on to it. In Portland, we'd started a tradition of "Starbucks Sundays" and now that we were back in Charleston, part of the Starbucks tradition involved scanning the real estate section of The Post and Courier. Property values kept going up. The homes in our old neighborhood were selling for more than we could afford.

One day, I saw a listing for a house close to our apartment. They were having an open house that afternoon. This listing would break our budget, but we just had to see it. A few hours later, Shawn and I stood in the back yard overlooking the golf course. Shawn put his arm around me, the way he had when we stood on the construction site two years earlier. We hadn't lost our ability to dream and visualize our life together. From my perspective, Shawn had fallen back into step, growing into his new role managing the production department at Channel 5 and enjoying his office with the window. I was still spinning my wheels.

✦

I went through the motions, but it eventually became more difficult to pull myself out of bed each day. I asked Randall to put dark lowlights in my hair. I didn't want to be a bright blonde anymore. I wondered, if I went to the doctor, would I be diagnosed with depression? It was hard to tell, because some days after I'd forced myself to get up and get going, I'd catch myself feeling hopeful, perhaps even happy.

One weekend in April, Channel 2 hosted its annual telethon to raise money to support children with birth defects and their families. When I arrived for my four-hour shift, the station buzzed with activity. The studio had been completely rearranged and set up to showcase several stages: the group of volunteers working the phones, the spot for local singers and dancers to perform, and the platform where businesses and organizations presented jumbo-sized checks to the charity.

Producers and directors worked from a basic rundown, but there were no scripts. We ad-libbed and listened for our next cue. I spent the morning following the producer's directions, moving from stage to stage, interviewing contributors and volunteers, introducing performers and asking the audience for donations. Then, I was assigned to sit at the main desk with the sports anchor, Brendan. It felt as fun and natural as it did when I worked on the morning show at Channel 5.

After my four-hour shift was over, I drove out of Mount Pleasant and along Interstate 26 toward my apartment. I felt like I was on one of those moving walkways at the airport. You're walking, but at super-speed, and it feels effortless. I couldn't remember a time that I'd felt so light, as if I were gliding down the highway, propelled by some good and magical force. I felt like myself. Not some imitation of myself. Not some stressed-out professional version of myself. Not an actor dressing up and playing a part, but like me, doing what I'm designed to do.

I'd enjoyed every moment of work that morning, and I realized that this was the type of communicating and storytelling I really loved. The kind that was positive, inspiring. The kind that shined the spotlight on people living from the heart.

A few days later, I told Greg how much I enjoyed hosting the telethon, and I'd realized the type of newsperson I wanted to be. Greg's solution was "to act the part I wanted to play." That entailed getting more involved in the community. Speaking to more groups. Building my own brand. All of that sounded very nice, but it didn't sound like "we're going to take you off the crime beat ASAP." What did I expect him to say?

A week later, Greg announced he was leaving the station and taking a news director job in another state.

✦

April rolled into May, and springtime in Charleston was in full bloom, which naturally lightened my mood. One day, my mom gave me a book called "Tuesdays With Morrie."

"You really ought to read this," she said.

One night after work, I poured a glass of red wine and filled up the bathtub. Once I started reading, I could barely put it down. I was captivated by the story of the author, Mitch Albom, a young, ambitious sportswriter who'd reconnected with his college professor, Morrie Schwartz. Morrie was dying of Lou Gehrig's disease, and during their visits each week, Morrie would offer Mitch a lesson and assign him simple tasks like pausing to admire the view from the window. Mitch's conversations with the dying man changed how Mitch viewed his life and his success.

This line reverberated in my mind for days: "If you accept that you can die at any time then you might not be as ambitious as you are," Morrie said. "The things you spend so much time on—all this work you do—might not seem as important."

I recalled a memory from childhood: I was lying in my grandparents' front yard on Marilyn Drive inspecting a blade of grass. I couldn't have been older than 6 years old. As I stared at the grass up close, it occurred to me that one day, I would die. I'm not sure why I thought of it or how I was able to process a thought like that at my young age. I only knew that the realization scared me, the truth that this life I was living wouldn't go on and on forever. I wondered what it would feel like to not be in my body anymore, to no longer be there, under that tree staring at the grass. I wanted to live a meaningful life. But what was I doing now? Was I really living? I read until the bubbles in the bath disappeared and the water turned cold.

✦

After that, I made some small changes to reduce my stress level. I tried to work out regularly, light more candles and indulge in more bubble baths. I also tried to have more romantic evenings with Shawn, even though they were becoming dangerous territory. After we split a bottle of wine, and then another, I recycled the same old conversation, saying my spiraling thoughts out loud: Why are things falling into place for you and not for me? What does this all mean? What do I have to do to get my life back?

This night, Shawn set down his wine glass. He took mine and placed it on the kitchen table. Then he grabbed my hand, pulled me out of my seat, and kissed me, more passionately than he possibly ever had. "None of that stuff matters. Just let it go."

He led me back to the bedroom, and for a moment, as we fell onto the bed, I felt myself letting it all go, giving in to him.

"I'm ready," he whispered.

I knew what "I'm ready" meant. Shawn was ready to have a baby. I'd recently gone off the pill, but we were still using protection with the understanding we'd try to get pregnant eventually. But Shawn meant he was ready right now. That night. This sent me into a full-blown panic. I pulled away and sat up.

"Shawn, no." His eyes revealed the hurt, the impact of my rejection. Shawn wanted me. He wanted to build a life with me. He wanted to have a family with me. Wasn't that what I wanted too? And suddenly, with my own eyes, I saw how he was inviting me into the life I wanted. Now, I was standing in my own way. I also knew that I couldn't accept his invitation. Not yet, not like this. "Shawn, I want to have a family with you. Just not now."

Back in college, during a trip home to Charleston, Shawn and I were walking along Folly Beach. I told Shawn that we needed to discuss what would happen if I got pregnant. "What would you want to do?"

"I'd want to have the baby," he said. "Think about it. Your mom had you."

My mom always told me that my conception was an accident, but my life wasn't a mistake. I was meant to be here. I wanted my child to feel that way too. I knew, as much as I wanted to say yes to Shawn, I wasn't mentally and emotionally healthy enough to grow, birth and care for a child. But I decided, in that moment, that one day I would be.

I'd lost people I loved. The world as I knew it had ended time and time again. I worked in a business where I raced against the sands of the hourglass every single day. Yet, I'd been walking around like I had all this time to figure it out. Time to get it right. Time to allow myself to be happy. Time to start living a full and joyful life, the kind of life that Morrie Schwartz talked about. Instead, I was going through the motions and struggling to make it through the day.

It was time for a change.

NEW LIGHT

A few days later, I set up an appointment with my primary care doctor. I told the receptionist I wanted to have a mole checked, one that had been on my back near my left shoulder since I was a child. I'd had it examined before and was told it was normal. But a concerned friend whose mother had battled melanoma encouraged me to go to the doctor again just to be safe. As I sat in the waiting room, I already felt lighter and a sense of relief. I knew I was there for another reason. I needed to talk to someone, but I didn't know how to tell the receptionist that.

Thirty minutes later, the doctor examined the mole and said it looked good. The edges were normal. She explained that removing it would leave a huge scar and for now, it would be best to keep getting it checked. And then she looked at me. Like she knew.

"Is there anything else going on?" she asked.

Like a child, I wanted to lay my head in her lap and let her stroke my hair. Instead, I kept my distance and proceeded slowly, giving her the CliffsNotes version of what had happened over the past year.

"Moves can be extremely difficult," she said. "It's one of the top five stressors." I think I had read that somewhere "And so, to move cross-country twice in one year, then adjusting to a new job ... that would explain a lot." And all this time I'd wondered what was wrong with me, pointing at all the ways I'd brought it on myself. "You know," she continued. "I have my practice, and I have my children. And it's not easy. I used to think I could have it all. Now I realize I have to make choices."

I have to make choices. What did it mean to have it all, anyway? I'd spent a lot of time wanting what other people had and shaping my life according to other people's standards and expectations. What did I want? I'd spent most of my life in motion. In Portland, I was forced to stand still. When we moved back to Charleston, I tried to go back and do what I'd always done. But I wasn't the same person anymore.

My doctor reminded me that I had choices. That was the same thing I told my mom when she confessed that she wanted to leave Portland and move back to Charleston. It's the same thing Darla told me that day in the makeup room. We live our life by making choices. And now, here was another professional, successful woman, not telling me to work harder and to suck it up. She was telling me she understood. But why was my doctor giving me a glimpse into her personal struggles? Maybe I wasn't as alone as I thought.

She gave me a moment to process what she'd said. Then she proceeded with her prescription. No medication. Just someone to listen. "Some people do well with talk therapy. Why don't we try that first?"

I said that sounded good to me. The doctor said she'd call in a referral and the psychologist would be in touch. I got in the car and headed back to work, already feeling better that I was doing something. I'd been trying so hard and for so long to figure out what was going on with me, but whatever it was, it had somehow gotten too big to deal with on my own. I needed help. Accepting that was a relief.

✦

"Are you OK?" the assistant news director asked when I returned to the newsroom later that morning. His question caught me off guard. How did he know? I remembered I'd told him I was getting a mole checked. He was simply being polite and clueless about the state of my mental health.

I told him I was fine. He gave me my assignment: A second court hearing for a man accused of accidentally killing two young girls with a shotgun in rural Berkeley County. A teenaged boy had been his intended target, compounding the tragedy, but the boy hadn't been hurt. It had happened on a Friday night months earlier, and I'd driven 45 minutes out to the scene in the dark, meeting up with the videographer who'd been out covering another story. When we got there, the crime scene had been cleared and I resorted to knocking on doors for interviews. No one wanted to talk, but at one point, family members invited me inside the trailer where they gathered to mourn. It was devastating. This court hearing was expected to be straightforward, a formality.

Court started at 2 p.m. and the station wanted me to go live at 5 p.m. I had some free time, so I searched the archives and found the scripts and video from when the story aired in November. I typed the anchor intros, saved them to the rundown and then went to lunch. I decided on a restaurant close to the station. I ordered a salad and got it to go.

The Channel 2 general manager had begun to enforce a "no eating in the newsroom" policy, and the entire staff was in a tizzy. What do you mean we have to eat our lunch in the break room? We're too busy! What if we miss something on the police scanners? We have deadlines! He held firm on the grounds that we were disgusting. Our desks were decorated with fast food cartons and empty drink cups, and the scent of onions and stale French fries wafted from the trash cans. He said, "If you don't have time in your day to stop and eat and take a break, something's wrong." So I drove back to the station and ate my salad—alone—on the back patio overlooking the pond. I sat outside in the quiet for 45 minutes. The longest and most relaxing lunch break I'd taken since I'd started the job.

When it was time to drive to court, I opted to take my car and follow the videographer in the live truck so I could head straight home after the newscast. On the road, my cell phone rang.

"Hi, Angie. This is Dr. Risa Mason. Dr. Hiott asked me to give you a call." Her voice gave no hint of judgment, and I wondered why, until now, therapy had felt so taboo.

"Yes, hi. Thank you for calling."

"So, what's going on?"

I told her what I told Dr. Hiott. After a series of "uh-huhs" and "ah, yesses" to indicate she was nodding and listening, she said, "What you're going through is very common." I wondered if doctors said that to make us feel better, or because most of us are harboring a great deal of stress and we're all trying to cover it up.

We talked for 15 minutes. We discussed her fee; she didn't accept insurance, but I could file the claim myself and get reimbursed. She offered the times she had available for appointments. We said goodbye when I arrived at the courthouse.

The courtroom was packed, filled with what appeared to be the entire population of the tiny rural town. The videographer set up near the front of the room, off to the side. I stood behind the last row of benches, out of the way, with my back against the wall.

Officers led the suspect into the courtroom, and we all rose for the judge. Suddenly, a fight broke out. The teenaged boy—the intended target who had escaped the fatal shots—lunged toward the suspect, and it was difficult to tell what happened next. It seemed like everyone was fighting, but the crowd was trying to restrain the teen. I froze in place, mouth agape. I didn't see a lead story; I only saw pain.

How do we ever break the cycle?

✦

A few days later, I sat in the waiting room of a townhouse converted into an office space for therapists, and the stairs creaked as a tan woman made her way down to greet me. The first thing I noticed was her shoes—sandals that revealed bright pink toenails. She was dressed in colorful, flowing pants and a sleeveless shirt, and her wavy brown hair was pulled back in a loose ponytail.

I thought about what I wore to work each day: the suit that I couldn't stop sweating through no matter how much deodorant I applied. And makeup. And hairspray. In the humid South, the only solution was to reapply. And reapply and reapply. At the end of the day, I was a sticky, dirty mess.

She led me up the stairs and into her office, and I sunk into the couch lined with fluffy pillows. The walls were a rusty orange, giving off a tropical vacation vibe. She sat in a plush chair across from me and a candle burned on the table next to her. The window above her desk was open. Tree limbs swayed in the breeze; I could hear the birds.

During the intake interview, she asked me questions about my childhood. I recited the facts, laying it out like bullet points, and I said, "But I've dealt with all that." That's not why I was there. We had more pressing matters to discuss.

She nodded and said we weren't going to explore those issues right away. "Right now, we're in crisis mode. We need to address what's happening right now."

"Well," I began. "I absolutely want to quit my job. My husband and I moved away to Portland and came back, and I know there's a lot of stuff going on with me, but that's the bottom line. I want to quit, but I'm scared." The words came out so quickly I surprised myself, and I gave myself a little imaginary high five.

"If you could do anything else, what would that be?"

"I think I'd love to work at a gym, maybe become a personal trainer or group fitness instructor." It's as if the answer had bubbled up from my subconscious, like one of those games when you're supposed to say the first thing that comes to mind, and you wonder where it came from. I thought of Edie, the hip hop dance instructor in Portland. I remembered how I watched her when I saw her later at the gym and discovered that she also taught step aerobics and body pump. I marveled at the ease with which she seemed to move through the world. I recalled my days as a high school cheerleader and the night I two-stepped with a stranger at the country bar. Moving my body had always been a gateway to feeling more alive inside.

"And," I said, "I want to write stories." I was on a roll now. "Not news stories. Personal essays, like the kind you find in Skirt! magazine." Once again, I felt shocked by my own words. How true they felt, as if the answer was always right there below the surface. I recalled how many times I'd flipped through each new issue of the local magazine, reading the personal stories written by women and stopping every time I saw an advertisement for a gym or Pilates studio.

The therapist smiled and said, "Why don't you do that?"

"I signed a contract," I said. "It's pretty intimidating."

"Have someone look at it. Get an attorney."

✦

When I left the session, on a whim, I drove into downtown Charleston to the waterfront. I stepped out of the car and admired the blue water and the seagulls flying overhead. I inhaled the salty breeze and made my way to the fountain walk, searching for a new, upscale health club I'd heard about on the radio.

I was searching for Tim. Tim was a well-known personal trainer I'd met and become friends with years earlier when

I worked at Channel 5. The commercial said I'd find him there. The gym showcased state-of-the-art equipment, high ceilings, windows for walls and an unobstructed view of the Charleston Harbor. The manager said Tim wasn't there, so I left a note asking him to call me.

I got back in the car and drove to North Charleston to visit my mom, who was off work that day. Minutes later, my cell phone rang. Not recognizing the number, I answered it.

"Hey, Angie, it's Tim! I must've just missed you."

I told him that I was in a life transition and would love to meet with him. He said he was leaving work in the next couple of hours. We made plans to meet for coffee later that afternoon.

When I arrived at Mom's, she greeted me at the door and said, "Angie, you look amazing."

I looked down at my attire: cargo pants and a white T-shirt. It occurred to me that I was dressed as casually as the therapist, but I didn't feel as vibrant. "Um, I'm not sure about that," I said.

"Your face. You're glowing."

"I am? Well, thanks." I wondered if stress—and the absence of stress—could really alter one's appearance. Mom made glasses of sweet tea and we went out to the back deck. I told her about the therapy session, stopping by the gym, and my upcoming meeting with Tim. "Mom, do you think I'm crazy? I have no idea what I'm doing."

"Angie, I've listened to you go on and on about work. You get upset about every little thing. I want to help, but I want you to make your own decisions and do what's best for you."

That's when I noticed how moving to Portland and back had changed her. When I was young, she may have pushed me to live a different kind of life than she had lived, and our signals got crossed many times. But she only wanted what was best for me.

"I feel good right now," I said, propping my feet up on the plastic patio table. I tilted my head back and stared at the sky. I'd put so much pressure on myself to succeed. I wondered if I was brave enough to do what I was about to do.

I thought back to a phone conversation we'd had a month earlier; around the time she'd given me the book "Tuesdays With Morrie." I'd called her from the newsroom; complaining about something, who knows what, and talking under my breath so my co-workers wouldn't hear.

"Angie, you need to know," she said. "You have more power than you realize."

I didn't really hear her that day, but now I did. Perhaps this was the thing she'd been trying to tell me—the thing she wanted me to know—all along.

PERFECT DAY

Sitting in Barnes and Noble on a weekday, when I should have been at work pushing a deadline, felt bizarre to me. I'd taken an approved personal day, but it felt like I'd cut school or broken out of jail. Tim, on the other hand, looked relaxed and confident. I took note of his dry fit workout wear, recognizing again my growing disdain for my closet filled with ink-stained suits.

I took a sip of my latte and said, "This may come as a surprise, but I'm thinking about changing careers. I'm thinking about leaving TV news and becoming a personal trainer."

He didn't seem surprised. Perhaps it was only surprising to me; I'd had a big day of saying bold things out loud.

"I think you'd be an awesome trainer," he said. He pulled a pen out of his pocket and wrote the letters NASM on a napkin. "This is the name of the certification I require for trainers at the fitness club."

Then he wrote down some numbers, starting with a personal trainer's average hourly rate. He said I could train five clients a day and match my $30,000 salary as a local TV news reporter.

"It would take some time to build the clientele," he said, "but you have the energy and the people skills to do it."

I sat and stared at the math. Five hours into what would have been a workday, I was just getting started. I was more attracted to how amazing it felt to even be considering this new path, that I was daring to think about doing something new. For the first time since—I didn't know when—it occurred to me that I had control over my career. What was stopping me from moving in this direction? For so long, I'd felt trapped. Here I was, drinking a latte in the middle of the afternoon on a weekday. I wasn't trapped.

"Have you ever read 'Who Moved My Cheese?'" Tim asked.

"No." I laughed before I could stop myself. "That's a strange name for a book."

"I know, but you should check it out."

I wondered about that. I'd overdosed on spiritual and self-help books back in Portland. It seemed silly to keep looking to books and other people's wisdom for guidance on what to do with my own life. Then again, I'd just spent an hour talking to a therapist.

Tim finished his unsweetened green tea, and I took a final swig of my sugary caffeinated treat and thanked him for his time.

CHAPTER THIRTY-FIVE

"I'll walk you to your car," he said.

When we got outside, Tim stopped in the middle of the parking lot. "What's your perfect day?" He blurted it out, like he intuitively knew a part of me was still on the fence. "Just think about it. How do you want to spend your days? How do you want to work? How do you want to live?" He paused for a moment, letting his words fill the space between us. "Whatever it is, whatever you see, believe in that. You can make it happen."

Did I hate my job, or did I want the things my job was crowding out? I'd written that in my journal once, and the question kept resurfacing. I certainly didn't hate everything about my job. There were plenty of things I liked. Not every day was terrible. Tim wasn't asking me to answer that question. He asked me to imagine my perfect day. Just allow myself to imagine it. I couldn't see it then, not all the way. But I knew that my perfect day included room to breathe.

"Tim, thank you," I said again, before collapsing into a dizzy embrace, awkwardly expressing the depth of my gratitude, for his kindness, his generosity, and for taking the time to encourage an old friend.

"I'll be in touch," I said, as I climbed into the car and waved goodbye. I sat for a moment and fiddled with the radio. Instead of putting the car in reverse and driving away, I turned off the ignition.

I ran back inside the bookstore and headed straight to the customer information desk. "Excuse me. I'm looking for the book 'Who Moved My Cheese?' Do you know where I can find it?"

✦

When I got home, I sat on my bed and opened the book. It was about 100 pages, with large font. It reminded me of a children's book, and it appeared, at first glance, to be about mice searching for cheese. Finding cheese made the mice happy. But along the way, some mice got lost. The book was a simple parable about change. I flipped the page and the words "What would you do if you weren't afraid?" leaped out at me, grabbing my attention. The question was— literally—the only words on the page. It was a question I'd never considered before.

The book already assumed that I was afraid. It didn't shame me for being afraid. The book gave me permission to stop pretending that I wasn't. I was reading the book because I was, in fact, afraid. The question simply asked: "What would you do if you weren't?"

I shut the book. I decided to take a walk. When I got outside and strolled down the sidewalk, I noticed the blue sky and felt the quiet rising up all around me.

Earlier, the therapist asked, "If you quit your job, what's the worst thing that could happen?" Would I plummet into poverty? Would the world end? Would my friends and family stop loving me? She told me to investigate my fear. Stare it down.

I realized one of my biggest fears—besides my big, scary contract that felt like a jail cell—was what other people thought about me. I didn't want anyone to think that I gave up on my career, that I couldn't handle it. I was afraid of disappointing my boss and co-workers, of letting them down. Still, I knew the answer. I knew the answer to the question as soon as I saw it.

If I weren't afraid, I would quit.

I would quit my job.

I would stop saying yes when I meant no.

I'd let go of the belief that I'd carried around my whole life: The belief that if I didn't perform—if nobody saw me—I didn't exist. I'd stop trying to prove my worth with a job description. I'd stop looking out into the world for confirmation that I was here, that my life was meaningful, that I mattered.

I thought back to the little girl I used to be, singing into the microphone of that jukebox-shaped karaoke machine. I can still see my mom's and grandparents' faces, glowing with so much love and adoration. When my family fell apart, performing became my way of surviving in the world.

Performing filled a void. Performing was my broken path to love.

You are enough. You are whole. Regardless of who sees you. Even if no one sees you. I knew those words were coming from someplace bigger than me. Someplace honest and someplace safe.

That night, I talked to Shawn. Our conversation started in the kitchen and eventually slid down to the floor, Shawn leaning against the wall and my back pressing against the cabinets. What a day! I told him about the appointment with the therapist, the visit with Mom and the meeting with Tim. I told him about the book Tim recommended and the question that had finally lifted the veil from my eyes. Shawn listened, like he always did, letting me talk until I was done.

He looked at me with the same sincerity he'd shown the night at Portland City Grill when he told me he wanted to stay married. "Angie," he said, "if you can succeed in a career you hate, just think about what you could do with something you love."

Shawn, my mom, and even my teachers in high school had believed in me. They always knew. But I needed to know. Maybe that's why I showed up in television station lobbies unannounced and knocked on all those doors—to prove that underneath my cheery persona I had some moxie, some grit. I didn't need to prove it to the industry gatekeepers or to my competitors. I needed to prove it to myself.

When I woke up the next morning, I didn't hit snooze. I got up and went straight to the shower. I knew what I needed to do.

✦

When I pulled into the Channel 2 parking lot, my heart was beating in my throat. I thought back to my interview at Channel 5 almost a decade earlier and recognized how the end of my career looked so much like the beginning. On the outside, I was calm, masking the sound of my heartbeat, the blood pulsing in my ears and the burning sensation in the pit of my stomach. I got out of the car. No turning back.

I walked inside the building and straight to the general manager's office. I knocked lightly on the door and asked if I could come in. I took a seat. "I'm here because," I paused. I started again. "I'm here because I need to resign."

"Oh," he said, clearly not seeing that coming. "Is it something we've done?"

"No, nothing like that," I said. I wasn't looking for someone to blame. "It's a personal issue," I explained, recalling language I got from the therapist. I needed words to help me say the thing that felt impossible to say. Getting less scripted, I said, "Lately, I've felt like I'm falling apart. This has everything to do with me."

We discussed my contract and the fact that I was breaking it. I told him that I wanted to leave the news business; it wasn't my intention to work for a competing station. I told him that I needed to go in a new direction, that I was thinking about becoming a personal trainer. "I hope that one day, if I ever run into you, I'll be able to tell you that I'm better—better than I've been in a long time."

"I hope so, too," he said. He didn't try to change my mind. He told me to call the human resources director about my resignation, and she'd give me guidance on the next steps to take. He said he would reach out to the corporate office and talk to them about releasing me from my contract. Getting released would require a new document that I'd need to agree upon and sign. He said we'd have to work out a way to part amicably. This is when I understood that day would be my last. He told me he wished me the best.

I walked out of the television station, and the glass door closed behind me. As I drove over the bridge, across the Cooper River, I felt the bittersweet mix of loss and acceptance. Dozens of good memories flashed before me. Early in my career when I worked at one of my first jobs in Savannah and ate green grits on live television during the famous St. Patrick's Day celebration. Scenes from my wedding on the nightly news. From the local fair to forest fires, from bank robberies to school board meetings, from hurricanes to the hype around the new millennium and Y2K.

All of those high fives and after-work beers with co-workers to celebrate another day of getting the story and making the deadlines, in the nick of time.

I blinked away tears as I smiled. It was so much easier for me to reduce an experience to good or bad. But to look back with no regrets, I had to be willing to take it all and appreciate how it coexisted. How it all worked together to illuminate the next step. This was the beginning of a new chapter. Months away from my 30th birthday, driving away from the dream and into the bright unknown, I'd finally become my own girl. It felt like the first day of my life.

LETTING GO

One of my friends was married to an attorney, and he agreed to represent me pro bono during the process of negotiating the release from my contract. The back and forth with my former employer felt upsetting at times, but having someone advise me opened my eyes to areas where I needed to push back. We stressed that I wasn't trying to break my non-compete agreement, but as it was, the release was limiting my ability to accept most work in my areas of training. My attorney explained that, yes, the employer had rights. But I did too.

We came to an amicable parting agreement. I agreed to a non-compete clause that stated I wouldn't immediately run off and start working for the competition. I didn't agree to sections that would prevent me from working in related professions, like producing and appearing in commercials. We worked it out. I bought my attorney friend a gift card to a fancy restaurant, a small token of appreciation. I'd pay attention the next time I felt uneasy. I wouldn't push those feelings aside. I'd know those feelings were trying to tell me something. I'd remember that I had the right to pause, to ask questions and to speak up. And, perhaps more radical, I could say no.

The day after I walked out of Channel 2 for good, I called the health club and asked for Tim. "Hey, guess what?" I said when he picked up the line. "I read 'Who Moved My Cheese?' Now I'm looking for a job."

"Oh, wow!" he said, chuckling. "I'll remember that the next time I recommend a book."

I got hired to work at the front desk at the health club and help with sales and marketing. I also got a free gym membership. I studied to become a certified personal trainer and learned how to use the gym's new, state-of-the-art exercise equipment. The gym had an upscale industrial feel, with brick walls, high ceilings and tall windows. I looked around and out toward the Charleston Harbor and marveled at this new world.

✦

According to the holistic nutritionist at the health club, the purpose of my time there was to "de-stress" myself.

"How long will that take?" I asked.

"About a year," she said.

I appreciated the prediction. It helped to have some idea about where I was headed. Reducing my stress level felt like a valid goal, a huge contrast from the past year where I rarely had time to exercise or even eat.

I continued to go to therapy. One day, I told my therapist that I was worried about running into my former co-workers in public. What would I say?

"OK, let's just imagine this. Imagine you're out somewhere. Where would you be?"

I said Rue de Jean, a restaurant in downtown Charleston. During my Channel 5 days, we'd go there on Friday nights.

She continued, "So imagine you're standing at the bar at Rue de Jean, and everyone you ever worked with shows up." She told me to name some people. "Imagine they all walk up to you, and Meredith says, 'Hey, Angie, what happened? Where did you go?'"

"I guess I'd say, 'Working at Channel 2 just wasn't a good fit. For my own well-being. I decided that I needed to move on.'"

She continued with the role-play, pretending to be Meredith. "Oh, so you're not in news anymore? Do you think you'll ever go back?"

"I'm not sure. I don't have any immediate plans to do that. Right now, I'm working at the new health club on the Charleston Harbor and getting my personal trainer certification."

"Do you like it? Are you happy?"

"Yes. Yes, I do. And yes, I think I am."

I realized that as I said it out loud, it was true. Or at least it was on the way to becoming true. I got to decide whether I liked the new path I was taking in life. I got to decide if I was happy. No one else had a say in that. It was my choice to make.

The therapist replied, "Do you see? Sometimes when you say something out loud, the fear loses its power over you."

As we transitioned out of crisis mode, the therapist returned to the initial intake questions. To move forward, she needed to know more about me and my story.

"Tell me about your parents," she said.

"My mom is Debbie. And there's my biological father, John. He was abusive and he and my mom split up when I was 3. He's sober now and we have a limited relationship."

I continued to lay out the facts like an autobiography. Or perhaps, an encyclopedia. I knew the story. I'd processed it and moved on with my life. I didn't see the need to dig into it again. "My mom married my stepdad Cam when I was in second grade, and he adopted me when I was 8."

"Are they still married?" she asked.

"He left when I was 13 ..." I stopped; the rest of the sentence caught in my throat, like I might choke. I let out an unexpected sob, and my face contorted. The ugliest of ugly cries. I covered my face with my hands, embarrassed.

No, mortified. "I'm so sorry," I said, between breaths. "I don't know what's happening."

"Don't be sorry," she said, getting up and handing me a tissue box. She sat back down in her chair as I tried to sink deeper and deeper into the fluffy couch. I needed to become invisible, to hide. "This is good," she reassured. "This is really, really good." How was this good? "You're feeling your feelings, Angie. It's OK to feel your feelings."

The only other time in my life I'd ever cried like this was during my sophomore year of college after my grandmother died. I was lying in the twin bed of my dorm room, trying to fall asleep, when thoughts of her flooded my mind. I couldn't erase her face, and the cruel truth taunted me. I'd never be able to hug her, to hear her voice again. The heat rose in my body and my chest caved in. I tried to wrestle down the grief, hold it in until it felt like my eardrums would pop. I cried out loud.

My roommate hopped out of bed and pulled me up and wrapped me in an embrace.

"I miss her so bad," I whispered.

My roommate didn't ask questions. She didn't say anything at all. She held me as I cried, until I felt like I could breathe again.

Not long after that, my grandmother showed up in a dream. She wore an ivory nightgown, and her hair was teased and set. Her makeup done. She looked like she looked on Fridays after her weekly appointment at the hair salon, or as she called it, the beauty shop. She told me that she loved me and that she was proud of me. She answered a question I couldn't ask, because this was one of those dreams where the words wouldn't come out. "I'm fine, sugar," she said with a bright smile. "I'm just fine."

The director of the funeral home had counseled my mom, uncle Bobby and me about the doorways we'd pass through—in no particular order—on the way to healing: denial, anger, bargaining, depression, and eventually, acceptance. The pamphlet he gave us said it would take a year. A year felt like an eternity and not long enough. I would never stop missing her. I wasn't sure that sadness would ever really end, even after acceptance, and I was right about that. But after that dream, I knew my grandmother was with me, always. I felt her spirit, around me and within me.

Inside the therapist's office, I continued to cry but felt myself settling down, as if a pressure valve had been released. My mind flashed back to Cam standing at the door, telling me he had to leave. The door closed. The 13-year-old version of myself stood there, stunned. No tears. I'd never fully grieved that loss, until now. That day in the therapist's office I cried for that young girl, on the brink of adolescence. Perhaps she was too young to feel the effects of that heartbreak. Perhaps she'd internalized it, or maybe she believed that she could carry enough love for both of them, for everyone. Maybe she simply distracted herself, turning her attention to the outside world—to the spotlight—trying to find a place to belong. That little girl was never, ever searching for fame. She was searching for home.

It was time to show her the way.

FINDING HOME

Six months after I left my job at Channel 2, on an early weekday morning in October, my cell phone rang. It was Tim. I smiled and picked up the phone to a round of "Happy Birthday" and applause and cheers from other trainers and staff members at the gym in the background.

"Thank you," I said, laughing.

"We didn't wake you, did we?" Tim chirped.

"No, I'm awake. My mom has been calling me before dawn on my birthday since I was in college. But I'm hanging up now. Thanks again. See you later."

I used to think that by the time I turned 30, I'd be the host of an entertainment news show in Los Angeles. If you'd told me that instead, I'd be a certified personal trainer, working at a gym with a picturesque view of the Charleston waterfront, I wouldn't have believed you. But there I was, living a version of my life I never planned.

I took vitamins and shopped for organic food. Each day, after I trained clients, I'd step onto the elliptical machine, pop in my ear buds and listen to music as I watched boats sail through the Charleston Harbor. As my body moved to the rhythm of the music, I could hear my mind working, churning up anecdotes and witty and poignant phrases. I'd hold those thoughts until I got home. Then, I'd open my journal and write them down.

✦

"I think I'm getting my life back," I told my therapist one day.

"Tell me more about that," she said.

I explained that I'd recently reconnected with a former colleague, and we were talking about doing public relations and marketing together, on the side. Our plan was to write press releases and help clients get media coverage to promote their services and upcoming special events. Recently, we had met for drinks. We'd chatted with the bartender, Damon, who also worked at the gym with me. Damon had a side hustle too.

"It was just so fun," I told the therapist. "I have new friends, work I enjoy, and things to look forward to again."

I thought she'd give me a gold star. Most improved patient. Instead, she said, "It's interesting. It seems like you're still looking for these things to fill you up, things that are outside of you."

Wait. What? Wasn't this the goal? To reinvent my life, and to like it? I was stumped. And yet, I knew she wasn't wrong. If I didn't have outside confirmation that I was OK, how could I be sure that I was really OK?

I noted how there was a sadness, a loneliness that continued to follow me around, and these feelings always seemed to come up during a yoga class that I'd recently started taking. The studio was located next door to the gym. The class was led by two instructors, a husband-and-wife team who were poster children for the benefits of a devoted yoga practice. They were, undeniably, glowing and gorgeous. While one instructor called the poses, the other walked around the room, adjusting our positions and helping us balance. Recently, I'd learned how to stand on my head, which required less thinking, more breathing. When I became aware of what I was doing, I'd panic and topple over. When I allowed my thoughts to pass by and "return to the breath," as the instructors advised, my toes rose effortlessly toward the ceiling.

At the end of one class, as I was lying on the floor on my back preparing for savasana, I stretched my arms out to the side, and my hand brushed against the hand of the female instructor. Before my reflexes kicked in and I had a chance to quickly jerk away, she patted my arm. Three times, gently. I felt an energy being transferred: kindness, goodness, compassion. It was as if she touched the loneliest, darkest, saddest part of me, simultaneously cracking me open and sending the message that everything was going to be OK. I turned my head away from her and closed my eyes, letting the lone tear fall. I continued to lay there in silence, allowing the emotions to pass through me, relaxing into the sadness rather than resisting it.

I understood what my therapist was saying. I thought about how, in high school, I devoted myself to cheerleading and the youth group. It wasn't that these places weren't good for me, it's that they became my escape. Even though I was running toward good places, I was still searching for everything I needed outside of myself. I'd look to my high-profile career to fill the void, and it worked for a while. Until it didn't.

✦

Delaine, our Realtor, and I had stayed in touch, and when she called me one day and said, "Girl, I am standing inside your next house," I knew it was the one.

The following day, Delaine and I pulled into the driveway of a pale green bungalow. The house was in the trendy Avondale area, two miles from downtown Charleston and within walking distance of shops and restaurants. Most of the houses on this street were built on slabs and made from cinder block, but this one was brand-new, with beautiful pine floors, crown molding, tile in the bathrooms and fresh paint. It was 1,000 square feet smaller than our first home, but after selling so much stuff when we moved to Portland, we no longer needed the extra space.

Shawn and I made an offer, and at the end of the month, we sat at the closing table once again. After we moved in, we found a Starbucks less than five minutes away and reinstated our Sunday tradition. Our new date night spot was also close, a tiki-themed bar named Voodoo. We bought flower boxes and two rocking chairs for the front porch, and I spent afternoons sitting there, rocking, absorbing the springtime air and reflecting on my position on the big map of my life.

✦

It had been one year since I quit my job at Channel 2. I wasn't sure if I was 100 percent "de-stressed" or if that was even possible, but I now understood that the balance I was seeking between the personal, the professional, the mind, the body and the spirit wasn't a deadline I needed to meet. It was simply a new way of living.

In many ways, life did return to the way it was before we left Charleston. Shawn still worked at Channel 5; our families and friends were nearby. I juggled working at the gym and my new side hustle doing PR. My days and nights were suddenly full again. I now had complete control of my work schedule, and my default was to fill up my time.

I'd continue to navigate this learning curve. Trial and error. Listening to my heart. One day at a time.

I admired my therapist, the way she appeared to have such clear boundaries around her schedule and how she conducted her business. That's the other thing I was learning about in therapy. Boundaries. To me, the word boundaries sounded harsh, like putting up walls to shut people out. My therapist presented it differently, saying that having boundaries was more like building a structure to support me, to protect myself from getting lost in other people's agendas. She said I needed boundaries to have healthy relationships, which was confusing because I'd always relaxed my boundaries to keep people close.

Sometimes, when the timer would ding, signaling the end of our session, it felt like being ripped through a portal. It was time to go. To be careful out there in the real world, with my hidden loneliness, where the boundary-pushers live. My therapist reminded me that a lot of the work in therapy happens outside of therapy. I had to go out into the world, vulnerable and exposed, and live my imperfect life.

✦

The meditations in yoga class helped, and especially on Thursday nights, when the instructors turned up the volume—literally. The hour-long class, appropriately named

"Rockasana," featured loud rock music. One night, the instructors guided us through a pose where we started on our backs, hugging our knees to our chest. Then, we started to rock, slowly, back and forth. As we allowed the momentum to build, we rocked bigger and bigger, picking up speed—literally rocking and rolling. Rufus Wainwright's cover of Leonard Cohen's "Hallelujah" played in the background.

I continued to rock back and forth effortlessly to the rhythm of the song and my breath until I was outside of my body and no longer in the room. I was on a stage, perhaps, and everything around me was black except for the spot where I was standing. It was as if I were awake inside a dream. Now, Mom, Cam and John were there too. One by one, they embraced me. Then, each other. Over and over, as if in a dance, we embraced again and again. We were tightly woven and unraveling threads all at once.

I knew I wasn't witnessing a reconciliation between them, at least not in the physical body. This was a glimpse of what it would look like, how it would feel, to be free from pain, as if I were getting a glimpse of heaven itself. I felt the weight lift, the release. I finally felt free to trust my own heart. I knew that it would always, in the end, tell me what to do. My awareness shifted back to class. The instructors lowered the volume and we prepared for the final resting pose, savasana. I rolled to my side, in a fetal position. My body exhaled. For quite possibly the first time, I breathed easy.

I had untangled myself from the net. I had cut myself out. And finally, I let it go.

✦

One afternoon, after I got home from the gym, I walked out on the front porch. I sat down in the rocking chair and looked out. I stared out into the open field across the road. Every now and then, a car whizzed by. I looked up at the surrounding tree branches and listened to the birds. The sky was a mix of puff clouds and blue.

My mind flashed forward, and I saw myself sitting in that same spot in the not-so-distant future. There I was, on another spring day, rocking an infant. The baby was swaddled in a blue blanket, a boy. He was my son.

I didn't yet know his name. I didn't know who or what he'd grow up to be. I couldn't see his face, snuggled against my arm. But I could feel him. I knew him already. One day, when he was old enough, I'd tell him my story. Maybe one day he'd hold the book in his hands. My story would not be his story; he would create his own. His world would be brand-new.

I would inevitably continue the work of healing. My son wouldn't get a perfect mom, or even a better mom, just a mom who was free. The cycle of pain was broken. I had broken the cycle.

When Shawn came home from work that night, I took him by the hand and said, "I'm ready."

THE WAY OUT

I kept writing. My essays were published in Skirt! magazine. When my first son was a toddler, I started a blog. When I was four months pregnant with my second child, I flew across the country to attend a writing retreat with the best name ever: Write the Damn Book. I wrote a few scenes. By the time my third child, my daughter, was born, I'd completed a first draft. The story was there—it was always there—but it didn't feel complete. I kept working on it and putting it away, again and again.

A few years later, Cam called and told me that he had cancer. I was driving down a two-lane road, a couple miles from home—the house I shared with Shawn and our three children. I stayed calm, eyes on the road, absorbing the impact of this news. He was about to turn 61.

There's one type of grief: the loss of a relationship or the death of a dream. And there's another kind when someone you love leaves this world. That kind of death feels so very final.

He told me he'd fight it, and he did. Even with chemotherapy and radiation, he never lost his full head of hair. It had turned gray at this point, but in my mind, it was still as dark as it was when he knocked on the townhouse door when I was little girl and said, "Hi, I'm Cam."

He didn't want my kids to see him dying. They knew him, but not really. He lived a private life. He refused to die in a hospital. He quietly slipped away, at his home, in his own bed. In his final days, he told me he'd made a lot of mistakes. I replied, "Well, you were my dad, and I'm grateful for that."

I apologized for not calling or coming around that much. It was never, ever because I didn't want to call or come by. "I just wanted to give you space," I said.

"Look around," he said, raising his arms, gesturing to the living room where we sat. "I have plenty of space."

In the final hours, he lay in bed with eyes open, awake, but perhaps not fully conscious. It seemed like he wanted to speak; maybe I was just imagining it. I didn't cry. I didn't beg him to stay. Instead, I rested my head on his chest, prayed that he could feel the love beating through mine.

I helped plan the funeral. I gave the eulogy. His friends from work, people I'd never met, told me that they'd seen my photo on his desk, that when he talked about me, he'd light up. After the funeral, his sister gave me a fireproof box. Inside I found newspaper clippings: the story about me making the All-Star cheerleading team in high school and our upcoming trip to London; a photo of me interviewing Armand Assante on the red carpet when the movie "The Hunley" premiered in Charleston; my engagement announcement. He'd saved the wedding invitation, the adoption papers. A story I'd written about him for school—Mom had mailed it to him. I never knew.

There are things I will never understand. Questions that will never go away. Answers that will never come. Life is a mystery. A maze. A dance.

Standing in the parking lot of the funeral home, my friend Meg gave me a book: "My Name is Lucy Barton" by Elizabeth Strout. "It's fiction," she said, "but the voice of the main character reminds me of you." In the novel, Lucy wrote of her attachments, her loneliness, her longings. Her desire to become a writer. My wise childhood friend had always known these things about me. She saw me before I saw myself. I knew it was time to return to the book that I first imagined when Shawn and I left Portland.

If Cam were alive today, I'd knock on his door, call without texting first. I wouldn't worry about bothering him. I'd break down the walls. But that's the grief talking, the bargaining. Things worked out differently, so I wrote about my longings instead.

Not long ago, at another writing retreat, on my birthday, I read sections of my story to a group of women. I've been going to this retreat for years; it's a safe and sacred space. These women listen and encourage me; they tell me that my story matters. Keep going. Their stories matter too. We stay at a lodge in rural Wisconsin. Most of the time, the lodge serves as a retreat center for families who've lost a child. During writing breaks, I walk the grounds. Octobers here are different than back in Charleston, where we have two seasons instead of four. Here, the leaves are a rainbow of fall colors, the air is crisp. All along the pathways, wooden signs with inspirational quotes are staked to the ground and hammered to trees.

The sign that gets my attention every time is the one with a quote by Robert Frost. It says: "The best way out is always through."

ACKNOWLEDGMENTS

Writing a book can sometimes feel like a solo endeavor, but when I pause to think about those who helped make this possible, I see a sea of faces: friends, family, colleagues and my online community. I was never alone.

To my weekly newsletter readers: Thank you for your comments that turn my musings into meaningful conversations. Because of you, the story continues.

To my mom, the first person to tell me that I could do anything: Publishing this book feels like a pretty big something—the truest thing. Thank you for your support as I explored and unraveled some of the most personal, joyful and painful parts of our family's past and for giving me space and grace to tell my story, through my eyes. Thank you for always seeing the bigger picture; the story isn't just about us. You understood that I wrote the book for those who might read it, resonate with it and feel inspired to free themselves too.

To Shawn: Thank you for knowing I had a book inside of me before I did and for believing in me even when I didn't. Through your patience, love and unwavering commitment you showed me that despite what the personality tests say about us, we do, in fact, want the same things.

To Dillon, Blake and Cate: Thank you for all the times you checked in on me and asked, "How's the book coming, Mom?" or the less subtle, "Why is it taking so long?" Thank you for all the times you said, "I'm proud of you." You three are the reason I never gave up. Supporting each of you as you find your own way in the world is my purpose, my most important and fulfilling work.

To Jude Morris: Thank you for making the students in your Honors English class keep a journal for a weekly completion grade or I certainly would've procrastinated. Filling the pages of that spiral notebook lit the spark that led me here—an author who has found her way back home to herself.

To Carolyn Matalene: Thank you for gently prompting me to rewrite that personal essay and to dare to tell the story from my perspective. Thank you for giving me an A that made me float across campus and for telling me that I could build a career around my writing ability. In your class, I discovered that the process of writing and revising makes me come alive, and you confirmed that what I was feeling was real.

To Mary Reynolds Thompson: Thank you for creating the writing retreat that inspired me to "Write the Damn Book." I produced exactly one scene that weekend, which was about my "rooftop epiphany" in Portland. One scene was enough to keep going.

To Nicole Lusiani: Thank you for instantly befriending me at that same retreat and telling me the next day about that amazing dream you had where my book was made into a movie and my mom was Sissy Spacek and I was Reese Witherspoon. (Wouldn't that be fantastic?) What you were really saying to me was that you connected with my story. At the time, I was four months pregnant with my second child, and you validated my deep belief that I wasn't pursuing a fantasy by trying to write a book.

To Kelly Love Johnson, Andra Watkins and Becca Finley: Thank you for reading, editing and helping me revise those early pages. You helped me get what author Anne Lamott famously calls the "shitty first draft" out of my head and onto the page. You always saw the gold. I couldn't have done it without you.

To Kerstin Martin: Thank you for generously offering your spare bedroom and a quiet, cozy space to think and write. I appreciate your hospitality and deep conversations about home. I'm so glad our "Angie Retreats" have become a tradition and that you witnessed this book coming to life behind the scenes.

To the Fisher Cats: Thank you for being a safe space to experiment with and share scenes that made me feel the most vulnerable and for reminding me that my story matters.

To Shauna VanBogart: Thank you for helping me realize that I'd lived in my "writing a book" identity long enough; it was time to finish it and experience the life waiting for me on the other side.

To Abby Green: Thank you for being the fresh set of eyes that snapped the last lingering pieces of this memoir into place and helped me finally feel ready to share this book with the world. I'm forever grateful to the internet for leading me to you: a writer and mom turned in-real-life friend.

To Kate Hopper: Thank you for being a kind, patient and encouraging editor, coach and friend. You helped me see what the story was really about—which was less about the end of my career and more about how performing had become my remedy for loss. You always knew where the story truly ended, and where it began.

To Chris Olsen and the team at Publish Her: I always hoped that I'd find a publisher who understood my story and was also an advocate for women's voices. From our very first call, I knew "Girl in the Spotlight" had found its home. Thank you.

ABOUT THE AUTHOR

Angie Mizzell is a writer, a mom and a former TV journalist. She's the author of "Hello Friday," a weekly newsletter where she explores ways to feel at home where we live, in our relationships, in our work, and within. She lives in Charleston, South Carolina, with her husband and their three children. For more information and to connect Angie, visit www.angiemizzell.com, and follow @angiemizzell on Instagram.

www.ingramcontent.com/pod-product-compliance
Lightning Source LLC
Chambersburg PA
CBHW071139130626
46553CB00004B/1439